W9-BON-065

Idiots in Charge

★ ★ ★

Other Books by Leland Gregory

What's the Number for 911?

What's the Number for 911 Again?

The Stupid Crook Book

Hey, Idiot!

Idiots at Work

Bush-Whacked

Idiots in Love

Am-Bushed!

Stupid History

Idiots in Charge

★ ★ ★

LIES, TRICKS, MISDEEDS, AND OTHER POLITICAL UNTRUTHINESS

LELAND GREGORY

**Andrews McMeel
Publishing, LLC**

Kansas City

IDIOTS IN CHARGE
★ ★ ★

Copyright © 2007 by Leland Gregory. All rights reserved.
Printed in Canada. No part of this book may
be used or reproduced in any manner whatsoever without written
permission except in the case of reprints in the context of reviews.
For information, write Andrews McMeel Publishing, LLC,
an Andrews McMeel Universal company, 4520 Main Street,
Kansas City, Missouri 64111.

08 09 10 11 TNS 10 9 8 7 6 5 4 3 2

ISBN-13: 978-0-7407-6970-2
ISBN-10: 0-7407-6970-7

Library of Congress Control Number:
2007927915

www.andrewsmcmeel.com

Attention: Schools and Businesses
Andrews McMeel books are available at quantity discounts with
bulk purchase for educational, business, or sales promotional use.
For information, please write to: Special Sales Department,
Andrews McMeel Publishing, LLC, 4520 Main Street,
Kansas City, Missouri 64111.

Plunging into History

★ ★ ★

At the November 24, 2003, Democratic National Committee debate in Des Moines, Iowa, former Illinois Senator Carol Moseley Braun offered an interesting analogy to the war in Iraq: "I'm reminded of the true story of my parents' worst argument. The toilet broke and there was water going everywhere. My mother sent my father to the hardware store; he came back with a new lawn mower." The audience laughed, and she continued: "That's what really happened to us in this country. They gave up a fight to protect the American people on behalf of a misadventure in Iraq." I'm not sure if the toilet story temporarily backed up her thinking, but I'm sure she was flushed with embarrassment afterward.

★★★★★★★★★★

"NOTHING IS MORE IMPORTANT IN THE FACE OF A WAR THAN CUTTING TAXES."

—Representative Tom DeLay (R-Tex.), speaking at an America's Community Bankers meeting, March 12, 2003

Spell-Checker

When Fred Pettry ran for the Charleston, West Virginia, City Council in 1998, he listed his party affiliation as "Democart" on his election form. Not a big deal, and Pettry won the election in spite of it. Four years later, when Pettry filled out papers for his reelection, he once again listed himself as a "Democart." What makes this story unique is that the other candidates also spelled their party affiliation that way—or as "Democrate" or "Demacrat." Obviously, poor spelling is a bipartisan issue, because two Republican opponents listed themselves as Republican and Repucican. Electing politicians who can't spell their party's name correctly can easily spell disaster for their constituents.

Immediately following a June 2002 Democratic Party meeting in Atlantic City, New Jersey, the challenger and the incumbent pulled knives on each other.

Leaning to the Right and the Left

San Francisco, California, Assemblyman Leland Yee has discovered a foolproof way to be on both sides of an issue at the same time. Yee cosponsored a state bill requiring all semiautomatic handguns leave a unique marking on every bullet fired, making it easier to trace the bullet back to the weapon. But in October 2006 when his bill came to the floor, Yee voted against it. That's right, he voted against his own bill, and it failed by three votes. According to the law, since Yee was not the deciding vote, he was allowed to go back and officially change his vote to a yes. So technically Yee can say he cosponsored the bill and voted for it, when the reality is that he cosponsored the bill and voted against it. Oh, Yee of little faith.

Missouri Republican Senators
Kit Bond and Jim Talent,
along with Republican Representative
Jo Ann Emerson, announced on
November 23, 2004, that they had
earmarked federal money for
three dozen projects in
southern Missouri, including
$50,000 for wild hog control.

It Is Better to Be Pissed Off...

During his unsuccessful race for county commissioner in Tallahassee, Florida, local weatherman Mike Rucker apologized for urinating in a voter's yard in October 2002. Rucker claimed that the incident was caused by a prostate problem, not that he was angry because the person refused to put a "Vote for Rucker" campaign sign in their yard. Now, if Rucker had been a yellow-dog Democrat, this activity might have made more sense.

"Now, tell me the truth, boys, is this kind of fun?"

—House Majority Leader Tom DeLay (R-Tex.), at the Astrodome in Houston, Texas, speaking to three young hurricane evacuees from New Orleans, September 9, 2005

Political Pole Dancing

★ ★ ★

His meager salary as mayor combined with the fact that his barbecue restaurant wasn't doing well forced Dale Sparks of Federal Heights, Colorado, to get a night job to make ends meet. In his new job, he *could* meet a lot of ends—rear ends, that is, since he took the position of doorman at Bare Essence, a local strip joint. In April 2006 the establishment was raided and a number of dancers were busted on charges of prostitution. Sparks was taken in for questioning and released without incident. "I don't know what goes on back there," Sparks said. Mayor Sparks soon announced that he would quit his job as doorman; once he's not working at a nudie bar, he'll be able to stay abreast of the city's concerns.

Water You Thinking?

A politician requesting funds for a bill is rarely newsworthy, unless the bill in question is a constituent's water bill, and the politician is funding it in exchange for sexual favors. That's just what happened in the second week of May 2006, when Troy Anderson, the mayor of Waldron, Arkansas, was arrested for soliciting sex from two women who fell behind on their water bills. Anderson, who was seventy-two years old at the time, was charged with two felony counts of abuse of public trust, plus four misdemeanor counts of patronizing a prostitute. The city council rejected a petition asking for Anderson's resignation, as that action, according to city attorney Ronald Killion, would be "completely premature." I recommend to Mr. Killion that in his next sexual misconduct case he not use the phrase "completely premature."

**"You're going to leave here in a body bag
if you keep this up."**

—Miami-Dade County, Florida, Commissioner Natacha Seijas to
Chairwoman Gwen Margolis for interrupting her during a budget
hearing; *Miami Herald*, September 20, 2002

A Long Stretch for a Short Ride

A story in the June 25, 2006, *Lexington Herald-Leader* reported that Kentucky Governor Ernie Fletcher is chauffeured to work every day in a limousine. The governor claims he needs this taxpayer-funded limousine and driver for security reasons and not because he's a lazy politician, even though the total distance from where he lives to where he works is a mere five hundred feet. At the same time the governor gets his daily free rides his administration is promoting a statewide fitness initiative encouraging Kentuckians to walk or bike more. Whatever the reason Fletcher has for being driven to work—fear or laziness—it answers this age-old riddle: Why did the governor cross the road? To get his limo to the other side.

Reach Out and Touch Someone

According to telephone records obtained by the *Tulsa World* newspaper and reported on June 22, 2002, Oklahoma State Representative Chad Stites, while speaking to a Tulsa official whose department was questioning him about code violations on his property, threatened that he would "neuter you sons of a [*sic*] bitches." The only person who wasn't offended by Stites's words was Bob Barker.

"I talk to those who've lost their lives, and they have that sense of duty and mission."

—Senator Jeff Sessions (R-Ala.) on American causalities in the Iraq War during Bob Gates's confirmation hearing for U.S. Secretary of Defense, December 5, 2006

Bow to Dow

★ ★ ★

Michigan Governor Jennifer Granholm issued a press release on March 28, 2006, announcing that in conjunction with the Michigan Economic Development Corporation, she had "helped convince [the Dow Chemical Company] to invest and create jobs in Michigan." Dow Chemical will receive a tax credit of $241,000 and $3.5 million in tax savings over twelve years to support the project. After Governor Granholm's self-congratulatory press release and the combined tax incentives to Dow Chemical, exactly how many new jobs were created? Four.

"You cannot go to a 7-Eleven or a Dunkin' Donuts unless you have a slight Indian accent. . . . I'm not joking."

—Senator Joe Biden (D-Del.) on the C-SPAN series
Road to the White House, June 17, 2006

Two Scoops Is Better Than One

★ ★ ★

Washington State Senator Joe Zarelli (R-Ridgefield) admitted to the *Columbian* newspaper in September 2002 that he had collected $12,000 in unemployment benefits in 2001–02 while simultaneously being paid $32,000 a year as a senator, which he didn't report. Zarelli claimed he'd "had no clue" he was supposed to divulge his legislator's salary, and he blamed the Employment Security Department for not discovering his mistake and explaining why what he was doing was illegal. Zarelli went on to say he thought he was being targeted by the agency not because he was cheating on his unemployment benefits but because he was a Republican. In Zarelli's defense, with the small amount of work state senators do, I can understand why he might have considered himself unemployed.

Say "Cheese"!

★ ★ ★

Ham and cheese are two things that go together, so it was only natural that when cheese was in trouble, ham was there to bail it out. The cheese is the Cuba, New York, Cheese Museum, and the ham comes in the form of pork-barrel spending. In 2005, New York Governor George Pataki criticized the legislature for spending money on ridiculous pet projects like cheese museums. But the cheese museum he referenced wasn't the one that received $5,000 in April 2006 from a fund controlled by Governor Pataki himself; it was the other one. And since there are two cheese museums in New York, it's only fair that the state cut the cheese money between them, because what's Gouda for one cheese museum is Gouda for the other.

"WE PICK UP STRAY ANIMALS AND SPAY THEM. THESE MOTHERS NEED TO BE SPAYED IF THEY CAN'T TAKE CARE OF THEIR [CHILDREN]."

—Charleston, South Carolina, Councilman Larry Shirley
on his solution to the city's youth crime problem;
Charleston Post and Courier, September 29, 2006

How Now Brown Cow

In April 2006 a dead cow floated lazily down the West Fork River in West Virginia and became caught on a tree branch at the West Milford Dam, causing a real stink for local residents. Concerned citizens made several cattle calls to local government agencies, all of which claimed that the cow wasn't under their jurisdiction. The bloated bovine was outside city limits, so it wasn't the town's responsibility; it wasn't a wild animal, and thus wasn't the state Department of Natural Resources' responsibility; it didn't pose an ecological danger, so it wasn't the Department of Environmental Protection's problem; the state Agriculture Department called it a local issue; and a regional water board washed its hands of any responsibility. Finally, on May 13, brave workers from the state Division of Highways, along with local volunteer firefighters, removed the carcass without cowering.

King of the Pork Sword

"I think with a lifetime appointment to the Supreme Court, you can't play, you know, hide the salami, or whatever it's called," said Democratic Party Chairman Howard Dean in an interview on the October 6, 2005, edition of *Hardball with Chris Matthews,* demanding that President Bush make public the records of his Supreme Court nominee Harriet Miers while she served as the president's legal council. I'm sure if Freud were alive he would love to analyze why Dean slipped and used the phrase "hide the salami" when talking about a female lawyer.

"If I would do another *Terminator* movie I would have Terminator travel back in time and tell Arnold not to have a special election."

—California Governor Arnold Schwarzenegger on November 10, 2005, concerning the special election he called in which all four of his ballot initiatives were soundly defeated

Name Caller Calling

★ ★ ★

On May 16, 2006, Boulder, Colorado, became the first city in the United States to allocate taxpayer money to establish a hate hotline. The city council approved spending $16,000 to create the hotline so that insulted citizens could complain about incidents of bias "based on their race, gender, sexual orientation, or other differences." Council members said the hotline wasn't to be used to help file criminal charges and that the calls might not even be documented, as there's no way to verify their authenticity.

OFFICIALS IN VERMILLION COUNTY,
INDIANA, WERE TOLD BY STATE HOMELAND
SECURITY AUTHORITIES IN JULY 2006
TO STOP USING THE SPECIAL EMERGENCY-ONLY
HIGHWAY MESSAGE BOARDS TO
ADVERTISE THEIR CHARITY FISH FRIES
AND SPAGHETTI DINNERS.

Tit for Tat

★ ★ ★

Brunswick, Maine, District 1 Town Councillor David Watson resigned from his position as council vice chairman on January 23, 2007, after unintentionally forwarding an e-mail to eighteen members of the New Elementary School Building Committee. The e-mail contained nine embedded images of topless women under the heading "This Is National Women's Breast Awareness Day." The only other text in the e-mail read, "Beats . . . Martin Luther King Day, doesn't it?" I bet he felt like a real boob after that.

In the 2006 federal budget, $365,000 was added for the Center for Rural Studies in Vermont by Senate appropriator Patrick Leahy (D-Vt.). Since 1992, $2 million has been appropriated for this research even though, according to Citizens Against Government Waste, "No formal evaluation of this project has been conducted."

Some Assembly Required

The 109th Congress (2005–06) has been nicknamed "the do-nothing Congress" as the members of the Senate met for 125 days, while the House met for only 93 days. However, a December 13, 2006, report by CNN notes that Congress did manage to pass 383 pieces of legislation—nearly a fourth of which involved naming post offices (for Ray Charles in Los Angeles; Ava Gardner in Smithfield, North Carolina; former Representative Shirley Chisolm in Brooklyn, New York; and Karl Malden in Los Angeles) and other federal structures. What was Congress's final action before adjourning? Renaming the Chesapeake and Delaware Canal Bridge after Delaware Senator William V. Roth Jr. I'm sure angry citizens have some names they would like to call Congress.

Mime Your Own Business

During his 2001 campaign, the premier of Quebec, Jean-Bernard Landry, suggested that the province increase spending by about U.S.$11 million to help local graduates obtain jobs in Quebec. What's so funny about this proposal? The money would go to clowns. Quebec's National Circus School turns out eight to ten graduates a year, who are quickly snapped up by circuses around the world. According to an article in the February 13, 2001, edition of the *Montreal Gazette*, Landry wants to increase the number of graduates to twenty-five in the hopes that more will join Quebec's own Cirque du Soleil. Of course, if the clowns can't get a job in the Cirque du Soleil, they can always get a job in government.

"I happen to be a supporter of earmarks, unabashedly.
But I don't call them earmarks.
It is 'Congressional directed spending.'"

—Senator Tom Harkin (D-Iowa), in the *New York Times*,
November 25, 2006

Dare to Care

★ ★ ★

"This idea that you come to school hungry—come on! It's crazy! It's just so they can bring in all these lunch programs, breakfast programs—next, it's going to be dinner! . . . That's not the job of the schools—to feed the children. Let them pay for it or let them bring their own."

—Ezola Foster, vice presidential running mate to Reform Party candidate Pat Buchanan; *Washington Post*, September 13, 2000

According to an article in the March 1, 2006, *Hartwell Sun*, Georgia State Senator Nancy Schaefer (R-Turnerville), speaking at an "issues day" event in February, stated that one reason illegal immigrants come to the United States and easily find work is because "fifty million" abortions have caused a U.S. labor shortage. "We could have used those people," she said.

A Swing and a Miss

Since climbing into the political ring in 1980, New Mexico Governor Bill Richardson has bragged about being a draft pick for the Kansas City A's (now the Oakland A's), sometime in 1966, or 1967, or maybe 1968 (he's mentioned different years in different interviews). But an investigation in the November 24, 2005, *Albuquerque Journal* uncovered the exact year he was drafted: never. "After being notified of the situation and after researching the matter," Richardson later announced to the press, "I came to the conclusion that I was not drafted by the A's." Although he threw a curve ball with his claim of being drafted, he knocked one out of the park in November 2006 when he was reelected as governor.

IN JULY 2006, THE LUBBOCK, TEXAS, CITY COUNCIL AND THE LUBBOCK COMMISSIONER'S COURT ADOPTED RESOLUTIONS URGING RESIDENTS TO PRAY AND FAST FOR RAIN.

Tow the Line

★ ★ ★

After discussing two competing bids for a city towing contract, the Bloomington, Indiana, City Council voted in July 2001 to renew its deal with Brown's Wrecker Services, even though Brown's intended to raise the per-car towing charge from $8 to $20. The other contract, which was rejected, came from the city's heavy-truck contractor, Joe's Towing. What was Joe's bid per car? Nothing. Joe's proposed to tow cars at zero cost to the city, but for some unknown reason, its offer was rejected. Seems like the City Council's rational thinking has been impounded.

New York State Senator David Paterson (D-Harlem), running for lieutenant governor, was quoted in a March 29, 2006, *New York Post* article as saying he now regrets introducing unsuccessful legislation for fourteen straight years (until 2001) to make it legal for suspects to physically resist police.

Down the Hatch

After reading to a room full of fourth graders at Jo Mackey Elementary School, on March 2, 2005, Oscar Goodman, the mayor of Las Vegas, Nevada, was asked by one wide-eyed youth what his hobbies were. "Drinking" was one the mayor mentioned. Another child asked the mayor what one thing he would want if he were stranded on a desert island. "A bottle of gin," the mayor replied. Goodman was neither shaken nor stirred about the ensuing controversy and stated, "I'm the George Washington of mayors. I can't tell a lie." During a press conference at city hall the following day, the mayor was asked if he thought he had a drinking problem. Goodman said, "Absolutely not. No. I love to drink." See? No problem.

Can't Tolerate Intolerance

"Why do they kill people of other religions because of religion? Why do they hate the Israelis and despise their right to exist? Why do they hate each other? Why do Sunnis kill Shiites? How do they tell the difference? They all look the same to me."

—Senator Trent Lott (R-Miss), on September 28, 2006, explaining why he isn't in charge of foreign policy

President Bush's education secretary, Margaret Spellings, was beaten on "Celebrity Jeopardy!" in November 2006 by Michael McKean, best known for his role as Lenny on the television show *Laverne & Shirley* and for the movie *This Is Spinal Tap.*

"Everybody" Doesn't Mean Everybody

★ ★ ★

An exchange between presidential hopefuls Richard "Dick" Gephardt (D-Mo.) and John Edwards (D-N.C.) during the January 4, 2004, Democratic presidential primary debate in Iowa sounded more like an Abbot and Costello routine:

Dick Gephardt: "Everybody up here, except Dennis [Kucinich], voted for NAFTA and voted for the China agreement."

John Edwards: "I didn't vote for NAFTA. I campaigned against NAFTA."

Gephardt: "Well, John, you weren't in Congress when NAFTA came up, so you couldn't vote."

Edwards: "But you just said I voted for it."

Gephardt: "I understand."

Edwards: "You understand?"

"I think I'd just commit suicide."

—Senator John McCain (R-Ariz.), on October 18, 2006,
regarding his possible reaction to the Democrats'
taking back the Senate in the November 2006 election
(They did; he didn't.)

A Candidate Who Really Sucks

Minnesota is no stranger to unique political candidates. I mean, just look at Governor Jesse "the Body" Ventura. But during the 2006 election Minnesotans had a gubernatorial candidate who was a real pain in the neck. Jonathon "the Impaler" Sharkey, who claims to be a real vampire, ran as the leader of the Vampyres, Witches and Pagans Party. His campaign promises included personally impaling child molesters, convicted murderers, and other wrongdoers on a stake on the front lawn of the state capitol. The sun came up quickly on Sharkey's dark side when the police were called to his apartment and a routine check turned up two outstanding felony warrants. If he's put in prison, he might have to worry about being impaled by something other than a stake through his heart.

Taking the Fun out of Funds

James McCutcheon had his campaign strategy all in place and was preparing an aggressive run for Texas state representative against his incumbent Republican rival. Things were bouncing right along, and when it was time to write a check to pay the filing fee for his candidacy, things continued to bounce. In this case, it was his check. Since McCutcheon's check was returned he was declared ineligible to run. McLennan County Democratic Party officer John Cullar wrote in a January 2, 2006, letter, "There was some sort of mix-up concerning a deposit to the account on which his filing fee was written." Our government works on a system of checks and balances; in McCutcheon's case, before he wrote the check he should have made sure his bank account was balanced.

JAMES EPPERSON JR. OF EDWARDS COUNTY, TEXAS, RAN UNOPPOSED FOR HIS COUNTY COMMISSIONER SEAT IN THE 2000 REPUBLICAN PRIMARY. EASY RACE, RIGHT? UNFORTUNATELY, EPPERSON WAS RULED INELIGIBLE TO SERVE SINCE HE'D VOTED IN THE DEMOCRATIC PRIMARY (A VIOLATION OF STATE ELECTION LAW), THEREBY MAKING IT ILLEGAL FOR HIM TO RUN AS A REPUBLICAN.

Sent to the Clink

Coleen Rowley of Minnesota ran for the United States House of Representatives in an attempt to unseat incumbent Republican John Kline. Political advertising can get a little rough, but on January 3, 2006, an image appeared on Rowley's campaign Web site that made Kline fly into a furor—or should I say a führer. In the photo Kline's head was superimposed over a shot of fictitious Nazi Colonel Wilhelm Klink, the prison camp commandant from the 1960s TV show *Hogan's Heroes.* Rowley's campaign manager blamed the incident on an overzealous volunteer who somehow didn't know it was a bad idea to associate Kline with the Nazi Party. (Or in the famous words of *Hogan's Heroes* character Sergeant Schultz, "I hear nothing. I see nothing. I know nothing!")

Walking Against the Wind

Antanas Mockus, the eccentric former mayor of Bogotá, Colombia, had an inspired strategy for improving civility in his city: mimes. You know, those annoying white-faced, silent people who can't seem to get out of an invisible box? In 2004, Mockus hired 420 mimes to ridicule unruly motorists, jaywalkers, pickpockets, and the like by taunting, insulting, or impersonating them, or holding up signs that read, "Incorrecto!" The result? The streets of Bogotá are now considered significantly safer, thanks to the silent guardians. Mockus did it without passing new laws, without stricter enforcement of the laws on the books, without increasing the size of his police force. He did it by using what we used to call "American ingenuity."

David Spellman became the mayor of Black Hawk, Colorado, on July 12, 2006, a week after pleading guilty to felony menacing and third-degree assault for pistol-whipping his wife and firing three shots in 2005.

The Scales of Justice

In October 1994, Deptford, New Jersey, politician Mike Mostovlyan told the *Philadelphia Inquirer* that he had not intended to mail two large, dead fish to his political foe, Deputy Mayor Bea Cerkez. Actually, said Mostovlyan, he had intended to mail the fish to a friend in Puerto Rico and a book to Cerkez and had simply mislabeled the packages. I'm not sure which stinks more, the fish or the excuse.

MASSACHUSETTS STATE SENATOR GUY W. GLODIS (D-WORCESTER) SENT OUT A FLYER IN JUNE 2003 THAT ANGERED MUSLIMS AND CIVIL RIGHTS GROUPS ALIKE. THE FLYER, SENT TO FELLOW SENATORS, SUGGESTED THAT TERRORIST ATTACKS COULD BE THWARTED IF CONVICTED MUSLIM EXTREMISTS WERE EXECUTED AND BURIED WITH PIG ENTRAILS.

Caught in the Headlights

According to the *Washington Post* (February 7, 2005), in January 2005, during a Senate Judiciary Committee discussion about class-action lawsuits and silicone breast implants, Oklahoma State Representative and physician Tom Coburn said, "I thought I would just share with you what science says today about silicone breast implants. If you have them, you're healthier than if you don't. That is what the ultimate science shows. . . . In fact, there's no science that shows that silicone breast implants are detrimental and, in fact, they make you healthier." Finally, the proof men have been awaiting for years.

"I asked him the most important question that I think you could ask—if he had ever seen *Caddyshack*."

—Minnesota Governor Jesse Ventura on meeting
with the Dalai Lama in 2001

Election Selection

There have been several famous kingmakers—including James Carville, Karl Rove, and Travis Greenwell. Travis who? An obscure and much-overlooked state constitutional amendment in Kentucky caused the terms of office of the four incumbents on the Loretto City Council to automatically expire in November 1997. Travis Greenwell was perhaps the only person in the small town of eight hundred to have read the voting literature, and he sent in absentee ballots with the names of his mother, his uncle, a friend, and the owner of a local hardware store for the council positions—and they all won. All except the hardware-store owner declined to serve, and you can bet that the city council's first act will be to rewrite that particular election law.

Bumper Dumper

★ ★ ★

"We have brave men and women who are willing to step forward because they know what's at stake. They're willing to sacrifice their lives for this great country. What I'm asking all of you tonight is not to put on a uniform. Put on a bumper sticker. Is it that much to ask? Is it too much to ask to step up and serve your country?" —Senator Rick Santorum (R-Pa.) in January 2006, suggesting to supporters that putting a Rick Santorum bumper sticker on their cars was a way in which they could serve their country.

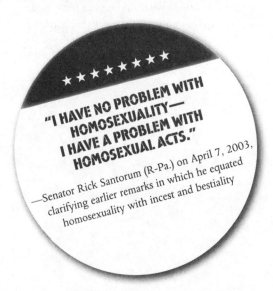

"I HAVE NO PROBLEM WITH HOMOSEXUALITY— I HAVE A PROBLEM WITH HOMOSEXUAL ACTS."

—Senator Rick Santorum (R-Pa.) on April 7, 2003, clarifying earlier remarks in which he equated homosexuality with incest and bestiality

The Good Ol' Days, Part I

Most people think our forefathers were gracious and eloquent men of class and honor—not like the members of Congress we have today. Well, I hate to burst the bubble, but here are verbatim excerpts from the Historical Summary of Conduct Cases in the House of Representatives, compiled by the Committee on Standards of Official Conduct:

 Representative Matthew Lyon (Vt.) was sited in 1798 for "disorderly behavior" because he spat on Representative Roger Griswold after an exchange of insults on January 30, 1798. A charge was added of "gross indecency of language in his defense before this House" on February 8, 1798.

 On February 15, 1798, Representative Roger Griswold (Conn.) and Representative Matthew Lyon (Vt.) were sited for "disorderly behavior" after Representative Griswold assaulted Representative Lyon with a "stout cane" on the House floor before the House was in session; Representative Lyon responded by attacking Representative Griswold with fireplace tongs.

In January 2003 the town council of Bend, Oregon, prohibited passengers from spitting and defecating on its transit buses and ruled to allow drivers to refuse service to riders who emanate "a grossly repulsive odor."

Smoke 'Em If You Got 'Em

During the November 4, 2003, Democratic presidential candidates forum sponsored by CNN and Rock the Vote at historic Faneuil Hall in Boston, Massachusetts, the candidates were asked if they had ever used marijuana. Here are their responses:

Howard Dean: "Yes."

Wesley Clark: "Never used it."

John Kerry: "Yes."

John Edwards: "Yes."

Joe Lieberman: "I have a reputation for giving unpopular answers in Democratic debates. I never used marijuana, sorry."

Al Sharpton: "I grew up in the church. We didn't believe in that."

Dennis Kucinich: "No, but I think it ought to be decriminalized."

Carol Moseley Braun: "I'm not going to answer."

Mike Taylor, a former salon owner and a 2002 Montana Republican U.S. Senate candidate, bitterly withdrew from the race in October, citing the fact that his Democratic opponent had run attack ads that, Taylor claimed, made him look gay.

Striking Out

★ ★ ★

To protest U.S. policy concerning the war in Iraq, Boston City Councilman Felix Arroyo announced in January 2003 that he would stage a liquid-only hunger strike. Later Arroyo changed his mind and stated that his protest would occur only in daylight hours, thereby permitting him to have dinner and, technically, breakfast if he woke up early enough. After further questioning from the press Arroyo said that he would strictly adhere to his hunger regime only on the second and fourth Fridays of each month. It seems like Arroyo is striking out against hunger strikes.

Sponsored by Senator Richard "Dick" Lugar (R-Ind.) in October 2005: S. 1413, a bill to redesignate the Crowne Plaza in Kingston, Jamaica, as the Colin L. Powell Residential Plaza.

But How Do You Really Feel?

In February 2003, Mayor Xochilt Ruvalcaba stood in front of an estimated crowd of two hundred yelling and screaming people protesting her term as mayor of South Gate, California, after she had been voted out of office by a special election on claims of corruption. To show her true feelings about her ouster, achieved in part by her nemesis, Councilman Henry Gonzalez, the thirty-year-old Ruvalcaba sucker-punched the councilman in the face. Gonzalez, it should be noted, was sixty-seven years old at the time and walked with the assistance of a cane.

IN A MAY 2003, SHUTESBURY, MASSACHUSETTS, TOWN MEETING, SEATING WAS DESIGNATED USING THE FOLLOWING CRITERIA: THOSE WEARING PERFUME OR AFTERSHAVE; THOSE WHO NEVER WEAR PERFUME OR AFTERSHAVE; AND THOSE WHO CLAIM THEY NEVER USE PERFUME OR AFTERSHAVE BUT FORGOT AND WORE SOME THAT DAY.

Pop a Cop

★ ★ ★

"For state representative, you don't have to tell where you stand on the issues," said Tom Alciere after being elected to the New Hampshire House in November 2000. One of his political issues, Alciere told the *Valley News* of Lebanon, is that he loves it when someone kills a police officer. Here is a verbatim excerpt from Alciere's Web site: "Maybe the USA will give up its war on drugs if Americans kill more cops. Nobody will ever be safe until the last cop is dead." Alciere resigned on January 10, 2001. If he'd had any smarts, he would have become a lyricist for a gangsta rap group.

"Tom Alciere is against sodomy laws because having a gay old time doesn't violate anybody's rights."

—From Tom Alciere's campaign Web site, http://tomalciere.us

Women's Suffrage or Sufferance

"**M**en should take care of women, and if men were taking care of women, we wouldn't have to vote," said Kansas State Senator Kay O'Connor (R-Olathe) when asked by the Johnson County League of Women Voters to attend its "Celebrate the Right to Vote" luncheon in September 2001. On the subject of the Nineteenth Amendment to the Constitution, which gave women the right to vote, Senator O'Connor was quoted as saying, "The Nineteenth Amendment is around because men weren't doing their jobs, and I think that's sad." The next time Ms. O'Connor decides to run for office she might consider being a candidate for the "Barefoot and Pregnant" Party.

In 2000 Republican Thomas Wesson ran unsuccessfully for constable in Dallas's largely Hispanic Sixth Precinct, despite changing his name to Tomás Eduardo Wesson.

Family Values

★ ★ ★

According to an April 20, 2006, article in the *Arizona Daily Star*, Republican Mike Harris contributed $100,000 of his own money to his gubernatorial campaign and promised to donate $150,000 more. Six months before that, Harris's wife had taken him to court because he was $22,500 behind in alimony and owed her $44,000 from the sale of their farm, the profits from which he had not disclosed. Harris, claiming near bankruptcy, had been able to convince the judge to cut his $2,000 monthly child-support payments for his seven-year-old son in half. When asked whether, since his financial situation had changed, he would start paying more than $1,000 in child support, Harris said, "For one kid, for a four-year marriage it's pretty darn generous." Looks like Hallmark lost another card sale for Father's Day.

Picture Perfect

★ ★ ★

"As you see here, and I think this is maybe the most important prop we'll have during the entire debate, my wife and I have been married forty-seven years. We have twenty kids and grandkids. I'm really proud to say that in the recorded history of our family, we've never had a divorce or any kind of homosexual relationship," said Senator James Inhofe (R-Okla.), gesturing to a prominently displayed family portrait while commenting on the Federal Marriage Amendment on June 6, 2006. I'm sure he meant that no one in his family has had a divorce or any kind of homosexual relationship—but it sure sounded like he was talking about himself and his wife.

Representative Gresham Barrett (R-S.C.) held a "Shag 'n' Eat" fund-raiser in June 2006. I hope this referred to the South Carolina state dance known as the shag, not the activity meant by Austin Powers's use of the term. That kind of a Shag 'n' Eat would be a hell of a fund-raiser.

Let Bygones Be Bygones

Trying to find a way to be all-inclusive, Kathryn L. Taylor, who was elected mayor of Tulsa, Oklahoma, on April 4, 2006, asked supporters of former Mayor Bill LaFortune for donations to help pay off more than $1 million in campaign debts. Jody Parker, Taylor's campaign manager, claimed the new mayor sent the letters to LaFortune supporters in an effort to bridge the gap between the parties. Taylor loaned her own campaign over $1 million, and it is that money that Taylor is hoping her opponents' supporters will help her raise. I guess it can't hurt to ask.

Detroit's city printing plant routinely prints flyers and business cards for city council members, but council member Kay Everett got some serious ink in March 2003. She had the printers publish a twelve-month calendar titled, *Hat's on Me in 2003*, in which each month featured a different photograph of Everett donning fashionable clothes and, of course, a hat.

A Real Pain in the Neck

As part of meeting his qualifications for the rank of Eagle Scout, a fourteen-year-old boy received permission from the Dallas, Texas, parks department to build and place three bat houses in the Glen Cove Park. You would think that politicians would be proud of a young man aspiring to better himself, but city council member Mitchell Rasansky flew off the handle when he heard about the bat houses. "He's not from North Dallas," Mr. Rasansky said. "He's actually from Transylvania." To top it all off, Rasansky showed up at city hall wearing a bat pin and a pair of plastic vampire teeth and further ridiculed the boy by referring to him as "Count Dracula." Despite public outrage over Rasansky's behavior, he was able to persuade the city's parks department to remove the three bat houses. The young boy received his Eagle Scout badge even with the flap Rasansky caused.

Class Dismissed

On April 13, 2005, Tom Craddick, the Speaker of the Texas House, taught a seventh-grade history class at the Mendez Middle School about our system of government. Craddick proclaimed to the twenty-five or so students, "Up there they have 400 and some on the House side, 454, and they have fewer on the Senate side, 60." Mr. Craddick should get a paddling and be sent to the principal's office, as there are 435 U.S. Representatives and 100 U.S. Senators.

"Obviously, being labeled the town from hell cannot be interpreted in any way as positive."

—Pikeville, Kentucky, City Manager Donovan Blackburn complaining about the 2005 episode of the A&E cable TV show *City Confidential* that depicted Pikeville as an undesirable town while focusing on a 1997 murder case

Klaatu Barada Nikto!

In the September 2000 Democratic primary for U.S. House from District 13 (Sarasota, Florida), Robert Salzberg finished a strong second even though six months earlier he had been charged with assaulting a police lieutenant. According to Salzberg, the officer was less of a cop and more of a RoboCop. "I started hitting him in the face over and over again," Salzberg told a psychiatrist. "But his face was weird. It was soft and it felt squishy and didn't move. I thought he was a robot at the time." Salzberg watched a videotape of the beating but claimed the events didn't correspond with his memory. The reason? A portion of his memory had somehow been removed. By the time Salzberg was found innocent by reason of insanity, the election was over. That was fine with Salzberg since campaigning, he said, had become increasingly difficult "because people think I'm crazy."

Forced Busing

★ ★ ★

Just as four school buses from Callaway High School in Jackson, Mississippi, turned onto Interstate 220 on April 28, 2006, Mayor Frank Melton, along with a police escort, flagged down the buses and had them pull over to the side of the road. As soon as the buses stopped, the mayor boarded the first one and started shaking hands and hugging the students. Melton explained his actions by telling the *Jackson Clarion-Ledger* that the previous few weeks had been "stressful" and that he's just "passionate" about kids and education. "I didn't do anything stupid or illegal," Melton said, although a state education official remarked that it was prohibited to interfere with a school bus except in an emergency. The biggest mistake Melton made was stopping the buses on their way home. Had he stopped them on the way to school and made all the kids late, he would have been every teenager's hero.

ON NOVEMBER 20, 2002, NEW YORK CITY
MAYOR MICHAEL BLOOMBERG ADMITTED
THAT HE WAS CONSIDERING OBTAINING
DEFUNCT CRUISE SHIPS TO LESSEN THE
NIGHTLY OVERCROWDING AT THE
CITY'S EMERGENCY SHELTERS.

Making a Big Splash

July in Ohio can get pretty hot, and there's nothing better than going for a nice refreshing swim in a pool. But in 2006, the water Georgetown, Ohio, Mayor John Jandes jumped into was politically hot after he used the local fire department to fill his personal swimming pool. "It's more than wrong," said one Georgetown resident. "It's outrageous." Jandes had his pool filled shortly after two fire department employees, having made the same request, were denied. I'll bet for Jandes the whole pool situation has become a big drain.

Mayor Jay Lee of Virgin, Utah, announced in October 2002 that there would be a mandatory $25 charge for any citizen who wished to address the town council during its public meetings.

The Political Circus

In October 2006, Kenneth Kahn announced that he was running for mayor of Alameda, California, and he wasn't just clowning around this time. Kahn, who is known professionally as Kenny the Clown, admitted he was a long shot, not because he's a clown (almost a prerequisite these days) but because he's never run for elected office before. "People ask me, 'Do we really want to elect a clown for mayor of the city?'" Kahn said. "I say, 'That's an excellent question.'" The answer to that question, however, was ultimately no. Kenneth Kahn got only 7 percent of the vote, losing out to Beverly Johnson. It's probably a good thing Kahn didn't become mayor, because the person who would have eventually succeeded him would have had some pretty big shoes to fill.

Hughes Whose

★ ★ ★

In 2002, Karen Hughes of Austin, Texas, then presidential adviser to George Bush, complained openly that Democrat Lloyd Doggett wasn't doing a sufficient job representing her in the U.S. House. Hughes bitterly accused Doggett of bias against her because of her association with the president and the fact that she is a Republican. Hughes soon realized why Doggett didn't represent her: he's not her representative. Her congressman was, in fact, Republican Lamar Smith.

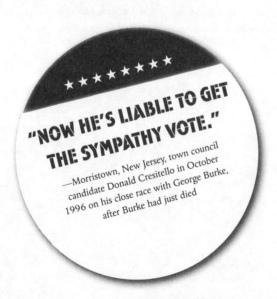

★★★★★★★★★

"NOW HE'S LIABLE TO GET THE SYMPATHY VOTE."

—Morristown, New Jersey, town council candidate Donald Cresitello in October 1996 on his close race with George Burke, after Burke had just died

Pack Your Trunk—You're Going Home

Raj Peter Bhakta, better known as the bow-tie-wearing contestant on Donald Trump's show *The Apprentice,* ran as a candidate for Pennsylvania's Thirteenth Congressional District in 2006. To show how border security was "a joke," Bhakta hired three elephants, a mariachi band, and a camera crew to shoot a commercial of them walking back and forth across the Rio Grande River on October 10, 2006. Ultimately the joke was on him, as the elephants were detained from crossing (and sprayed for ticks), the commercial was never shot, and Bhakta was defeated during the election. So, to sum up in the words of the immortal Donald Trump: You're fired!

Please Hang Up and Try Your Call Again

In case of a national emergency, you can rest comfortably knowing that a secret homeland security hotline is in the office of every governor in the United States. But Delaware Governor Ruth Ann Minner is tired of the hotline because, as she said in Washington, "Every time that phone rings, it's telemarketers." In an article in the June 15, 2006, *USA Today,* Miner said that when her line rings, "It's someone offering a time-share condominium or the latest deal for a long-distance phone provider." So Minner and other annoyed governors did what is suggested to citizens to ward off telemarketers: they placed the homeland security hotline on the "Do Not Call" list.

IN CHELMSFORD, MASSACHUSETTS,
THE TOWN COUNCIL DEBATED IN APRIL 2003
WHETHER TO OPEN THE MEETING WITH THE
PLEDGE OF ALLEGIANCE OR NOT. THE LOGICAL
PROBLEM SOON AROSE THAT SINCE THE
COUNCIL WAS ALREADY IN DEBATE, THEY
COULD NOT TECHNICALLY "OPEN" WITH
THE PLEDGE ANYWAY.

Hippo-crites

★ ★ ★

We all know the symbols of the elephant and the donkey in politics, but what about the hippo? "People remember hippos," said Mayor Mike Fowler of Hutto, Texas. The mayor is referring to the dozen or so 725-pound concrete hippopotami dressed in brightly colored clothes and hats that line the streets of the small Texas town of Hutto. But not everyone is hip to Hutto's hippos. "It's just stupid," said Murray McDonald, former president of Hutto's chamber of commerce in August 2003. "It's totally embarrassing is what it is." The only thing the town folks agree on is they're glad the mayor didn't like octopi.

★★★★★★★★★

The campaign slogan for the newly elected sheriff of Aiken County, South Carolina, in May 2003 was

"MIKE HUNT / ACCESSIBLE FOR YOU."

Booze It or Lose It

In the 2006 federal budget, $5.6 million was added by the House for the Gallo Center. According to its Web site, "The Ernest Gallo Clinic & Research Center (EGCRC) was established in 1980 to study basic neuroscience and the effects of alcohol and drug abuse on the brain." This earmark was buried in the defense budget, even though the EGCRC never mentions anything related to defense research. But who's going to wine over a few million anyway?

"What we really expect out of the Democrats is for them to treat us as they would like to have been treated."

—House Minority Leader John Boehner (R-Ohio) January 4, 2007

Double-Standard Operating Procedure

"We must take a strong stand against drugs, and I support strict punishment for individuals involved in the possession or distribution of illegal drugs," wrote Senator Richard Shelby (R-Ala.) in a letter to the father of a man sentenced to life in prison without parole even though no drugs, no money, and no physical evidence were produced and the man's accuser later recanted his testimony. Five years later, on July 24, 1998, Senator Shelby's son Claude was arrested in the Atlanta airport after arriving from London with thirteen grams of hashish in his pocket. He paid a $500 fine on the spot, pleaded guilty to a misdemeanor possession charge, performed forty hours of community service, and was on probation for one year. He spent not a single hour in jail. The lyrics from the song "Forunate Son" by Creedence Clearwater Revival that go "I ain't no senator's son" couldn't be more apropos.

Monarch of the Covenant

★ ★ ★

In December 2006 a coalition made up of the League of Polish Families Party, the Polish Peasants Party, and the forty-six Members of the Parliament from the ruling Law and Justice Party signed a petition proposing their candidate for king of Poland. But Poland is a republic ruled by an elected president and hasn't had a king since 1795. So who do these political parties want as their king? Why, the king of kings, of course—Jesus Christ. The Catholic Church, however, is cross about the idea of having Christ the King as Christ of Poland and has publicly denounced the proposal. I'm not sure Jesus would want the job as king anyway—the last time someone placed a crown on his head it wasn't very comfortable.

Nall Y'All

★ ★ ★

Loretta Nall, the Libertarian Party write-in candidate for governor of
Alabama, told reporters on October 23, 2006, that she purposely
shows a lot of cleavage in order to attract voters so they will stop and listen
to her political agenda. She also made available T-shirts bearing a photo
of herself in a plunging neckline and images of her political opponents.
The verbiage on the T-shirts reads, "More of these boobs and less of these
boobs." Her campaign wasn't just about titillating matters. There was also a
lot of talk about her foreign policy—people kept saying, "Nall's got quite
Iraq" and "Wow, what Iraq!"

According to an October 18, 2006, report on **KOCO**-TV in Oklahoma City, Bill Crozier, running for state school superintendent, proposed that school desks be made out of thick, used textbooks to stop bullets in case of an armed intruder and that new textbooks come with Kevlar covers.

A Plant Stand

★ ★ ★

The mayor of Bijeljina, Bosnia, Mico Micic, will work with a group of citizens to erect a massive monument to honor its most important product—cabbage. "We have agreed to the plans to erect a monument to cabbage," Micic said in November 2006. "It is the vegetable that feeds the people in this region and is important. It deserves recognition." I hope they decide to gild the cabbage monument; that way they can have gold-leaf cabbage.

"I stand by what I [wrote]."

—Rochester, Minnesota, mayoral candidate Pat Carr, admitting that he had posted complimentary messages about himself on a newspaper's Web site, *Star Tribune*, August 29, 2006

Pennies from Heaven

★ ★ ★

During the November 2006 elections in Alaska, Dona Highstone had stiff competition for a position on a rural school board, and the vote ended up a tie. State law requires a tie vote to be settled by the tossing of a coin. Highstone called heads, but the coin landed on tails. Highstone's opponent, unfortunately, wasn't there to witness the toss in her favor, as she had died earlier that day. But rules are rules, and the deceased Katherine Dunton was elected to the Adak school board. I've heard of people being bored stiff at a school board meeting but never of a school board stiff.

A Different Kind of Cover-Up

★ ★ ★

Randy White, up for reelection to the West Virginia state senate, decided in October 2006 to remain in the race despite newly published photographs showing White and a group of nude men covered in body paint. Instead of whitewashing over the situation, White admitted that the photographs were from a time two years earlier when he'd had a "personal identification situation." Voters appreciated his honesty (and maybe some liked the photographs), and when the final vote was tallied White had won.

During the August 8, 2006, episode of *The Bleepin Truth* on Tampa, Florida's public-access station, Republican guest Tony Katz threw a chair at county commission candidate Joe Redner, hitting him in the head. Katz had called Redner a liar, and Redner had responded by calling Katz "fat."

Give Her a Hand!

Following a televised debate on October 22, 2006, U.S. Representative Barbara Cubin (R-Wyo.) approached Libertarian candidate Thomas Rankin, who has multiple sclerosis and is confined to a wheelchair, to offer her hand—but not in friendship. "If you weren't sitting in that chair, I'd slap you across the face," Rankin claimed Cubin said. The *Billings Gazette* reported that Cubin "later apologized, saying she may have been influenced by listening to too much Rush Limbaugh." Limbaugh had earlier stated that he would slap actor and Parkinson's disease sufferer Michael J. Fox "if you'd just quit bobbing your head." Even with all this, Cubin was still reelected to the US House of Representatives— now, that's a real slap in the face.

Brown Sugar

Korinne Barnes was running for the North Kingstown, Rhode Island, school committee when an article about her MySpace.com personal listing became public. Not only was Barnes concerned about the school system, she was also "smart, sexy, fun" and a "voluptuous chocolate sister with a big booty." People visiting her site could read her personal diary entries, such as the one where she wrote she was looking forward to a weekend of "Sex, drugs and Rock and Roll." In another entry she discussed her plans to stay drunk and "out of control" on an upcoming trip. She was persuaded to take down the site in September 2006, but by then the damage was done, and she soon decided to drop out of the race. Too bad— she sounded like she would have had a great time in politics.

"Katherine Harris is the horse we're going to ride to the finish line, and it's time for us to saddle up."

—Florida State Representative David Rivera (R-Miami) on the selection of Katherine Harris as the Republican nominee to run against Senator Bill Nelson, May 2006

Sloop of War

★ ★ ★

The mayor of the town of Almere, Netherlands, Annemarie Jorritsma, appeared on Dutch national TV in October 2006 demanding "extra benefits" for soldiers serving abroad—a broad. Jorritsma suggested that Dutch prostitutes be sent to the two thousand or so soldiers stationed in Afghanistan and Bosnia, as a stress reliever. "The army must think about how their soldiers can let off some steam," Jorritsma said. The idea of "war whores" has been endorsed by the Dutch sex workers union and, more than likely, the two thousand or so soldiers stationed in Afghanistan and Bosnia.

FLORIDA STATE SENATE CANDIDATE
RANDALL TERRY, WHO RAN ON A
FAMILY-VALUES CAMPAIGN, ADMITTED ON
AUGUST 21, 2006, THAT THE FAMILY PHOTOS
IN HIS CAMPAIGN DIDN'T REALLY CONTAIN
THE WHOLE PICTURE. THE PHOTOS ARE MISSING
HIS TWO OSTRACIZED ADOPTED CHILDREN—
THE ONE WHO IS GAY AND THE ONE WHO
GAVE BIRTH OUT OF WEDLOCK.

Get a Grip

★ ★ ★

During his reelection campaign, the mistress of Republican U.S. Representative Don Sherwood of Pennsylvania not only confessed to their twenty-nine-year affair but also accused him of beating and strangling her. Sherwood decided to run television ads to fight the negative impact about his affair and possible abuse. "While I'm truly sorry for disappointing you," said Sherwood in a commercial, "I never wavered from my commitment to reduce taxes, create jobs, and bring home our fair share." The ad continued with "Should you forgive me, you can count on me to keep on fighting hard for you and your family." I don't know if the word "fighting" was the best choice for an accused abuser, but Sherwood couldn't put the stranglehold on the election and lost to Democrat Chris Carney. I'm sure Sherwood was all choked up.

"Now, wait a minute, wait a minute, they may be misleading, but they are his answers."

—Senate Judiciary Committee Chairman Arlen Specter, at John Roberts's Supreme Court confirmation hearing, after Senator Joe Biden said Roberts's remarks were "misleading". September 13, 2005

Going from Here to There in Sixty Seconds

★ ★ ★

House Speaker Dennis Hastert (R-Ill.)told Rush Limbaugh in October 2006, after the Mark Foley (R-Fla.) debacle, that he's making America safe from child sex predators, the Democrats, and other bad people. "We're trying to build better protections for these page programs. But, you know, this is a political issue in itself, too, and what we've tried to do as the Republican Party is make a better economy, protect this country against terrorism—and we've worked at it ever since 9/11, worked with the president on it—and there are some people that try to tear us down. We are the insulation to protect this country, and if they get to me it looks like they could affect our election as well."

Wow, I bet all the congressional pages feel safer now, don't you?

Doesn't Fall Far from the Tree

★ ★ ★

"These signs divert people away from the danger. This is a lot cheaper than having a no-win, no-fee solicitor taking us to court," said Worcester, England, council parks and cemeteries manager Ian Yates. The signs to which Yates was referring aren't placed by open manholes or exposed electrical lines—they warn about two pear trees. City officials began to worry that the two pear trees in Cripplegate Park were a threat to the citizenry because of the potential of falling pears. So in October 2006, signs reading, "Warning, pears falling!" were screwed into the trees' trunks—even though the trees have been in the park for fifty years without any incident of fatal fruit fallout.

During a stimulus-package debate, Senator John Breaux (D-La.) wrote a note and taped it on a congressional elevator. It read, "STIMULAS NEEDED!"

Full-Court Press

"Where we do get into challenges sometimes . . . we have the interlopers. . . .You might have correspondents who have not covered military affairs before, who don't really understand what it is they're dealing with."

—Pentagon Spokeswoman Victoria (Torie) Clarke,
Fox News, April 4, 2002

"Torie Clarke, the Pentagon's chief spokeswoman, freely admits that her previous knowledge of the military was 'next to nothing.'"

—*The Washington Post*, October 15, 2001

In 2001, right outside the Capitol building,
Representative Tom Lantos (D-Calif.) drove over
a thirteen-year-old boy's foot and then left the scene.

He's Nut Like the Rest

Campaigning can take a candidate to all sorts of places—retirement homes, schools, police stations, and, in one case, a mental health facility. Donovan Brown resumed campaigning in October 2006 after his mother had him committed to a two-week involuntary stay at a mental health facility. The Democrat nominee for a Florida house seat was diagnosed with obsessive-compulsive disorder, schizoaffective disorder, depression, anxiety, and panic attacks. Fortunately, the voters weren't crazy about having Brown as their representative, and they elected Republican Will Weatherford instead.

Hold the Pickle, Hold the Lettuce . . .

Texas Representative Betty Brown cooked up a whopper of a resolution in November 2006, officially declaring Athens, Texas, the birthplace of the hamburger. "It's not just our claim and what we say," she said. "The history is very well documented." But when Wisconsin Representative Tom Nelson heard the news, he flipped, because his resolution declared the town of Seymour, Wisconsin, as the official home of the hamburger. "Seymour is the hamburger capital, period," he said. Although the burger wars may remain a flame-broiled issue for years, the inhabitants of Hamburg, Germany ("Hamburgers") quietly sit on their buns and shake their heads in disbelief.

Harold Gunn of Houston, Texas, lost his race for state representative in the 2000 Republican primary after it was revealed that in 1983 he not only wrote but also appeared in a nudie flick entitled *The Great Texas Show*. Among other scenes, the film featured a naked woman jogging and a woman slathering herself with motor oil.

A Hot Tip

In the United States, someone caught taking a bribe is usually fired, arrested, suspended, or warned, but in Russia you might "burn in the flames of hell." The Russian government is using a mass leaflet-mailing scheme to warn citizens about what to do if they are asked for a bribe from any official—education, health, or the police. The leaflet, sent out in September 2006, quotes a passage from the Koran: "Both the giver and taker of a bribe will burn in the flames of hell." If this is true, then citizens of the United States should consider building an escalator for members of Congress—one that just goes down.

"The report speaks for itself. It's a very good report. It's a very long report. I haven't read the report yet."

—British Member of Parliament Keith Vaz; BBC Radio, *The World at One*, 2001

Knees Up, Mother Brown

"Her skirt was very short, and Josh found himself mesmerized by her perfectly shaped, silken legs with kneecaps that reminded him of golden apples—he couldn't remember having been captivated by kneecaps before—and her lustrous thighs. He tore his eyes away from Bianca's legs with the utmost difficulty."

—excerpt from the novel *A Time to Run* by Senator Barbara Boxer (D-Calif.)

"If you don't get those cameras out of my face,
I'm gonna go 8.6 on the Richter scale with gastric emissions
that'll clear this room!"

—Congressman James Traficant (D-Ohio), to photojournalists
covering his House ethics subcommittee hearing,
the *Washington Post*, July 25, 2002

The Wrong Fount

We've heard the stories of images of Christ appearing on refrigerator doors, Mother Teresa on a cinnamon bun, and the Virgin Mary on a grilled cheese sandwich. But when the people of Wadowice, Poland, saw water miraculously spewing from the base of a statue of Pope John Paul II, they knew it was divine intervention. Pilgrims traveled from all over the hometown of Pope John Paul II to drink at the "miracle fountain," filling up bottles of the holy water and reveling in a "godly experience." But town mayor Eva Filipiak, in a July 2006 article in *Nowy Dziennik* (Polish Daily News), soon evaporated everyone's sacred water rites and explained the source of the H_2O: the council has installed a pipe beneath the statue. "It was just supposed to make the statue look prettier," Filipiak said. This incident has given the Polish government their very own Watergate.

Are You Familiar with the Penal Codes?

At a congressional hearing in February 1994, the then director of the U.S. Fish and Wildlife Service, Mollie Beattie, argued with Alaska Congressman Don Young about exempting Alaska natives from laws protecting ocean animals. Beattie expressed her concern that seals, polar bears, and certain other animals were being slaughtered solely for their gall bladders and reproductive organs, which in some Asian countries are considered delicacies or aphrodisiacs. Young's temper flared and he grabbed a prop he had brought along and started slamming it into his hand as he spoke with Beattie—the prop was an eighteen-inch-long walrus penis. At least I hope he didn't tell Beattie he had a bone to pick with her.

According to a February 15, 2001, article in the *San Francisco Chronicle*, San Francisco Mayor Willie Brown felt forced to get a restraining order against an Elvis impersonator who had been hound-dogging him for a meeting to discuss how to rid the city of panhandlers and liberals.

A Real Chowderhead

Representative Patrick Kennedy (D-R.I.), the son of perennial Senator Ted Kennedy, is very outspoken. Unfortunately, he's usually not understood. Here is a verbatim question by Patrick Kennedy to the secretary of the navy in 1999 on how to eliminate racial intolerance from the military as reported in the *Weekly Standard* on June 7, 1999: "So what happens is, things don't get reported because, you know, let's not make much to-do about nothing, so to speak. One of the worries I have about, you know, a really zero-defect mentality with respect to defect—I'm not talking now—I mean everyone can acknowledge that if there's a little bit of extremism, I'm not saying that isn't just grounds for, you know, expulsion from the military. But how do we address the broader issues. . . . Can you answer that in terms of communication?"

Don't Quit Your Day Job

United State senators are very busy people—they write speeches, they write bills, they even write songs. Well, not all of them write songs, but one of them, Senator Orrin Hatch (R-Utah) has written what he calls a "patriotic rock song for children." Okay, everybody, start stomping out that two-four beat:

> America rocks! America rocks!
> From its busy bustling cities
> To its quiet country walks
> It's totally cool, it's totally hot
> I mean it's like right there at the top
> America rocks! America rocks! America rocks!

Someone needs to shut the hatch on Orrin.

"[You should] turn the sheriff loose and arrest every Muslim that crosses the state line."

—Representative Saxby Chambliss (R-Ga.) meeting with emergency responders in Valdosta, Georgia, on reducing terrorist threats, November 19, 2001

Meeting the Needs of the One

★ ★ ★

Sitting in on a meeting has got to be one of the most boring things one can do—unless, of course, that's what you're paid to do. According to a June 2000 *Chicago Sun-Times* report, Connie Peters's sole job was to serve as an "observer" at two state water-management meetings a month. For that she received $23,000 a year from the state. The report estimated that in the fifteen years she's held this position she's earned $185,000. The reason she's made so much for doing so little is that, for some unknown reason, the legislature has continually raised her compensation. When Peters started, in 1985, the job paid $150 a year. It looks like Illinois's water management is going to have a hard time managing its water if it keeps flushing money down the drain like this.

★ ★ ★ ★ ★ ★ ★ ★ ★ ★

"MY WORDS TO HOWARD DEAN ARE SIMPLE— SHUT UP."

—Representative Earl Pomeroy (D-N.D.) on Howard Dean's opinion of the war with Iraq, December 9, 2005

★ ★ ★ ★ ★ ★ ★ ★ ★

Don't Ask, Don't Tell, Don't Translate

"For some reason, the military seems more afraid of gay people than they are [of] terrorists, but they're very brave with the terrorists. . . . If the terrorists ever got ahold of this information, they'd get a platoon of lesbians to chase us out of Baghdad."

—Representative Gary Ackerman (D-N.Y.) on February 8, 2007, explaining that since dozens of foreign-language translators were fired because of the administration's "Don't Ask, Don't Tell" policy, Condoleezza Rice has no right to complain about the current lack of translators available for Iraq

"I'm saying that nobody knows what humiliating treatment is. What does it mean?"

—National Security Adviser Stephen Hadley on why U.S. terrorist interrogators need Congress to "clarify" the prohibition in the Geneva convention against "outrages upon personal dignity, in particular, humiliating and degrading treatment," September 18, 2006

Crazy Like a Fox

★ ★ ★

In the presidential election of 2000, Pat Buchanan's Reform Party running mate, Ezola Foster, a longtime opponent of most government social programs, admitted that in order to get California workers' compensation benefits, she submitted a false document in 1996. Foster claimed to have had a "mental illness" that entitled her to draw money for a year before her retirement as a typing teacher in 1997. When the issue of her mental stability came up during the campaign, Foster claimed her "mental illness" was worked out "between my doctor and my attorney. It's whatever the doctor said that, after working with my attorney, was best to help me." Foster founded the organization Black Americans for Family Value and is the author of the book *What's Right for All Americans*.

Hooch to Hoosegow to House

★ ★ ★

Connecticut State Representative Kevin Ryan refused to resign from the legislature after pleading guilty to a DUI and, because he was a recidivist drunk driver, he was sentenced to four months in jail on September 6, 2001. The five-term Democrat said, "I accept full responsibility for my actions," but he announced that he intended to conduct state business from his jail cell and return to the assembly after he'd served his time. I'll bet the other convicts were insulted when they were forced to share their cell with a politician.

"I have to confess, it was hard for me to concentrate in the conversation with Condoleezza Rice, because she has such nice legs."

—Israeli Prime Minister Ariel Sharon on his first meeting with Rice, in 2001

The Marriage Mirage

"The homosexual marriage lobby, as well as the polygamist lobby, they share the same goal of essentially breaking down all state-regulated marriage requirements to just one, and that one is consent. In doing so, they're paving the way for illegal protection of such practices as homosexual marriage, unrestricted sexual conduct between adults, and children, group marriage, incest, and, you know, if it feels good, do it."

—Senator James Inhofe's (R-Okla.) remarks on the Senate floor about the Federal Marriage Amendment, June 6, 2006

"I'd rather be at home making love to my wife while my children are asleep."

—Senator Joe Biden (D-Del.), the first Democrat to announce that he was exploring a run for president in 2008, explaining to a gathering of his leadership PAC on June 23, 2006, that he doesn't lust after the executive office

Great Scott!

At the February 21, 2001, county commission meeting in Wichita, Kansas, Commissioner Ben Sciortino objected to the proposed purchase of Scott paper towels for $15,000 more than a competitors brand. Despite the obvious price discrepancy, commissioners Betsy Gwin and Tim Norton wanted to prove to Sciortino that Scott was still the "Common Sense on a Roll" paper towel. They poured some water on the commissioner's table and, in a classic TV-commercial moment, tested the absorbency of each towel. The Scott brand sucked up the spill, and Sciortino sucked up his pride and allowed the purchase to go through.

Getting Railroaded

★ ★ ★

In the 2007 federal budget, $4 million was added by Senate Appropriations Committee Chairman Ted Stevens (R-Alaska) for the Northern Line Extension. The new railroad line will provide a direct route from North Pole, Alaska (pop. 1,597) to Delta Junction, Alaska (pop. 812), a distance of eighty-two miles. When members of Congress spend our tax dollars on useless pork projects like this, we ought to run them out of town on a rail.

"[This is] a place that would be pretty much like the place that I would have grown up in, I think, if I had have grown up here."

—Alan Keyes, on the Chicago neighborhood he moved to in order to qualify as a candidate for U.S. Senate in Illinois, 2004

Same Dance—Different Party

Representative Jim Moran (D-Va.) speaking in front of 450 people attending the Arlington County Democratic Committee's annual Jefferson-Jackson Day dinner, lambasted the Republican "culture of corruption" and blasted the practice of earmarks, the insertion of a line in a bill that designates funding to specific projects in the congressperson's home district. Shortly after Moran expressed his moral outrage at this process, he promised supporters at a June 9, 2006, gathering, "When I become chairman [of a House appropriations subcommittee], I'm going to earmark the shit out of it."

REPRESENTATIVE JIM MORAN (D-VA.) CAME
UNDER FIRE FOR SUPPORTING $37 MILLION
IN EARMARKS FOR "PROJECT M," WHICH
THE PENTAGON STATED HAS NO MILITARY
VALUE AND IS A WASTE OF TAXPAYER MONEY.
ACCORDING TO CITIZENS AGAINST GOVERNMENT
WASTE, THE OWNER OF PROJECT M'S PRIME
CONTRACTOR, VIBRATION & SOUND
SOLUTIONS LIMITED, HAS GIVEN $17,000 TO
MORAN'S CAMPAIGN. I WONDER IF THE "M"
IN PROJECT M STANDS FOR "MORAN."

Speak of the Devil

★ ★ ★

On November 5, 2001, Carolyn Risher, the mayor of the small town of Inglis, Florida, issued a devil of a proclamation—or, actually, an anti-devil proclamation. Risher's official proclamation reads, "Be it known from this day forward that Satan, ruler of darkness, giver of evil, destroyer of what is good and just, is not now, nor ever again will be, a part of this town of Inglis. Satan is hereby declared powerless, no longer ruling over, nor influencing, our citizens." Defending her position against proponents of the separation of church and state and people who were playing devil's advocate, Richer responded, "If I had thought I was doing something wrong, I would have not done it." Which, I think, is a very devil-may-care attitude.

"TANZANIAN LEGISLATOR WANTS ERRANT INVESTORS SPANKED"

—Reuters headline, April 6, 2006

Lucy, You Got Some 'Splainin' to Do

★ ★ ★

On January 8, 2007, FBI agents knocked on the door of the home of Chicago Alderman Arenda Troutman—for thirty minutes. They finally broke a window to conduct a warranted search and found a warm paper shredder, an unregistered handgun, white powder, and Alderman Arenda Troutman. Troutman explained that the white powder wasn't drugs but a dietary fiber she uses to cleanse her bowels. "You do it like a shake. You drink it. It explodes in your intestines and makes your bowels move," she said. "It's not a laxative because laxatives make you run off and they're not good actually." Troutman was arrested in connection with a federal investigation into bribery charges. The voters explained their frustration with Troutman by voting her out of office.

The Lame Blame Game

★ ★ ★

"Well, I think if you look at what actually happened, I remember on Tuesday morning picking up newspapers and I saw headlines, 'New Orleans Dodged the Bullet.' Because if you recall, the storm moved to the east and then continued on and appeared to pass with considerable damage but nothing worse." —Homeland Security Secretary Michael Chertoff, explaining where the real blame for the government's mishandling of Hurricane Katrina should be directed: at the media; from *Meet the Press*, September 4, 2005

2004 presidential hopeful Dennis Kucinich (D-Ohio) held up a pie chart to illustrate his point about a bloated Pentagon budget—during a debate that aired only on National Public Radio.

The Good Ol' Days, Part II

Here are more excerpts from the Historical Summary of Conduct Cases in the House of Representatives, compiled by the Committee on Standards of Official Conduct. These tales make modern Congressmen seem like pussycats.

 Representative William J. Graves (Ky.) and Representative Henry Wise (Va.) were sited for "breach of the privileges of the House" after Representative Graves killed Representative Jonathan Cilley (Maine) "in a duel over words spoken in debate; Representative Wise acted as a second" (February 24, 1838).

 Representative Philemon Herbert (Calif.) was arrested for manslaughter on May 8, 1856; he was imprisoned prior to trial and acquitted in July 1856.

 Representative Preston S. Brooks (S.C.) assaulted Senator Charles Sumner (Mass.) on the Senate floor after the Senate had adjourned for the day (May 22, 1856).

 Representative Lovell H. Rousseau (Ky.) assaulted Representative Josiah Grinnell (Iowa) with a cane outside the Capitol for alleged insult spoken in debate (June 14, 1866).

Unbridled Registry

In November 2006, as Arkansas Governor Mike Huckabee was preparing to leave office, he took the time to set up a wedding registry at two department stores, which might lead one to believe that Huckabee was getting married. But Huckabee had been happily married to Janet Huckabee for thirty-two years, so why did he set up two registries? Was he having an affair? Nope. Arkansas law prohibits gifts to public officials of more than $100, with a few exceptions—wedding gifts being one of them. I wouldn't be surprised if Huckabee set up a registry for a baby shower next.

In the 2001 mayoral election in Belleville, Illinois, incumbent Mark Andrew Kern was reelected mayor over challenger Mark Alan Kern without a single complaint of voter confusion.

Wash and Wear

In August 2001, Montana Governor Judy Martz answered her door and found a member of her staff, chief policy adviser Shane Hedges, covered in blood and in a state of panic. He told her he had been involved in a single-car accident and that the passenger in his car, Montana House Majority Leader Paul Sliter, had died. Martz took pity on the frightened young man and did what anyone would do in that situation: she washed his clothes. The police who were collecting evidence from the accident scene didn't learn about the laundered clothes until months later. Hedges was sentenced to community service and six months in a halfway house for negligent homicide and driving while drunk. But I'm sure that with good friends like Governor Martz, Hedges's record, like his clothes, will be wiped clean.

A Fairy Tale Come True

★ ★ ★

"We undressed and he kissed me. It was the first time in my life that a kiss meant what it was supposed to mean—it sent me through the roof. I was like a man emerging from 44 years in a cave to taste pure air for the first time, feel direct sunlight on pallid skin, warmth where there had only ever been a bone-chilling numbness. I pulled him to the bed and we made love like I'd always dreamed: a boastful, passionate, whispering, masculine kind of love."

—former New Jersey Governor James McGreevey, the first openly gay governor, from a passage in his book *The Confession* about Golan Cipel, the man he made New Jersey's homeland security adviser despite the fact that Cipel had no experience and was a foreign national

The campaign letterhead for the 2002 Tony Sanchez for Governor campaign in Texas read,

"TONY SANCHEZ FOR GONERER."

A Picture Is Worth a Thousand Words

"I know I was having problems when a lady in New Hampshire came up to me and she asked if she could have her picture taken with me, and I said, Really? Do you want to send this picture to your kids? She said, No, I just need to finish out the roll."

—Senator Orrin Hatch (R-Utah) on January 27, 2000,
citing one of the reasons he decided to withdraw from the 2000 presidential race

"We're no longer a superpower. We're a super-duper power."

—Representative Tom "the Hammer" DeLay (R-Tex.),
during an interview with Fox News in 2002, explaining why
America must overthrow Saddam Hussein

Suffer the Little Children

"Regardless of the fact of whether I'm guilty or unguilty, there are no children at the county legislature," said Richard Hobbs, who ultimately lost his campaign for the Westchester County, New York, legislature as a candidate from the Right to Life Party. Hobbs was explaining to a reporter in November 2001 why his being a twice-convicted pedophile wasn't relevant to his campaign.

Hobbs, who is also a professional clown, was back in the news a few years later when a judge ordered Westchester County to pay him $2,500 for violating his rights by refusing to allow him to perform his clown act in front of children at a local amusement park.

Beam Me Up, Scotty, There Are No Signs of Intelligent Life on the Planet

"This president has listened to some people, the so-called Vulcans in the White House, the ideologues. But you know, unlike the Vulcans of *Star Trek*, who made the decisions based on logic and fact, these guys make it on ideology. These aren't Vulcans. There are Klingons in the White House. But unlike the real Klingons of *Star Trek*, these Klingons have never fought a battle of their own. Don't let faux Klingons send real Americans to war."

—Representative David Wu (D-Ore.), in a speech to Congress,
drawing a comparison between Bush's advisers and
warmongering Klingons, January 10, 2007

"My number one goal is to not go to jail."

—Congresswoman-elect Michele Bachmann (R-Minn.), during "freshman orientation" for new members of Congress, November 13, 2006

Two Two-Bit Politicans

Minnesota Governor Tim Pawlenty and Colorado Governor Bill Owens had a "playful fight" over the design of their respective state commemorative quarters. George Washington will be on the front of each quarter, but the design of the tail, or reverse, side is decided upon by the individual states. "Would you ask [Pawlenty] what's going on with his quarter?" Owens said in June 2005. "That's one ugly quarter" because of the "big mosquitoes on it." Pawlenty flipped over Colorado's quarter because he claimed it had "some subliminal messaging . . . depicting Governor Owens in the buff." Owens countered that he was "surprised Tim Pawlenty could say the word 'subliminal.'" I think both of these penny-ante governors should be drawn and quartered, don't you?

Lubbock, Texas, Mayor David Miller sent an e-mail to nearly fifty city churches in October 2006 requesting that their congregations pray for the media to cover him fairly.

Spam-a-Lot

★ ★ ★

"Spam is an annoying, intrusive form of e-mail that almost all of us receive but few of us want," said Florida Attorney General Charlie Crist. So when he decided to run for governor he touted his crusade against spammers and how he helped stiffen the law against unsolicited e-mail. Then on December 21, 2005, in order to garner support for his candidacy, Crist began sending out campaign e-mails based in part on addresses obtained from the state's Web site. But Crist's political director, Arlene DiBenigno, defended her boss by claiming, "It's not spam. It's political speech." So the Monty Python skit could go: "Spam, spam, spam, spam, baked beans, spam, spam, spam, and political speech."

One Off the Frist

"I question it based on a review of the video footage which I spent an hour or so looking at last night in my office. She certainly seems to respond to visual stimuli," said Senator Bill Frist (R-Tenn.), during a speech on the Senate floor, explaining how he'd diagnosed Terri Schiavo's condition by looking at a video on March 17, 2005—even though she had been in a persistent vegetative state for fifteen years. When Schiavo died, on March 31, 2005, her autopsy revealed that she couldn't respond to visual stimuli because she was blind.

"WHICHEVER. CLOSE ENOUGH," SAID MINNESOTA GOVERNOR JESSE VENTURA ON FEBRUARY 2, 2000, SHRUGGING OFF HIS INABILITY TO REMEMBER WHICH ROOSEVELT SAID, "THE ONLY THING WE HAVE TO FEAR IS FEAR ITSELF." VENTURA HAD GUESSED TEDDY; THE REPORTER HAD REMINDED HIM THAT IT WAS FRANKLIN.

The Check's in the Mail

Jose A. Riesco, a campaign spokesman for U.S. Repesentative Lincoln Diaz-Balart (R-Fla.), decided that pleading incompetence was the best way out of a sticky situation. On December 20, 2000, Riesco told the *Miami Business Review* that forty-five illegal campaign checks totaling nearly $30,000 were refunded immediately after they were discovered, as Representative Diaz-Balart had promised and as required by law. But, strangely, none of the forty-five refund checks were cashed until eight months later, giving Diaz-Balart full use of the illegal campaign contributions through the end of the election. Why did it take so long for the checks to be received and cashed? Somehow every single one of the forty-five checks got lost in the mail. "Poorly addressed, things like that," Riesco said. Diaz-Balart was reelected to another term as a congressman; with the horrible postal service he received, he was lucky he wasn't dependent upon absentee ballots.

Valhalla or Bust

Getting into the spirit of April Fool's Day, the mayor of Cedar City, Utah, dreamed up a far-fetched story to publicize the town's festival on April 1, 2003. He related the tale of an island controlled by the Vikings in the tenth century that had been uprooted by a Pacific Ocean volcano and floated to a point near Cedar City. By virtue of a nineteenty-century treaty, the United States had hoodwinked the Vikings out of all rights to the island's artifacts but allowed them to continue to participate in the April festival. The mayor was completely surprised when he later received a letter from several residents of nearby St. George who claimed to be Viking descendants and angrily demanded "their" artifacts back. When the mayor explained that the story was all make-believe, the nonsensical Norsemen claimed that the whole thing was a cover-up. I guess that would make them Thor losers.

"So we're pro-panties—it's on the record."

—Gretna, Louisiana, City Councilman Vincent Cox, commenting on the council's decision to repeal an earlier ban on the throwing of women's underwear from Mardi Gras carnival floats, April 16, 2000

The New Man of La Mancha

An October 19, 2003, *Boston Globe* article profiled New Bedford, Massachusetts, city council candidate Raimundo Delgado, describing him as a well-liked political fixture and a dreamer in the tradition of Don Quixote. Like the classic hero who dressed in rusty armor and jousted with windmills, Delgado has his own giants to conquer—mainly his freely disclosed bipolar disorder and his two involuntary stays at a mental hospital. Delgado's political proposals included plans to create a "city underwater"; to "free the dogs, the sheep, the goats"; to grow a tropical forest on what is presently Route 18; and to give raises of $10,000 to numerous city employees. He lost the council election (as well as an earlier mayoral election), although he did receive 1,100 votes—thereby outpolling an opponent with schizophrenia. If you listen carefully, you can hear another windmill crashing to the ground.

In 2000, Mr. Will Wynn promised
that he "will win" a city council seat in
Austin, Texas. True to his word,
Will Wynn won.

Not a Member of a Steering Committee

On December 8, 2003, U.S. Representative Bill Janklow (R-S.D.) was convicted of second-degree manslaughter after he sped through a stop sign and killed a motorcyclist. Jurors were not informed of Janklow's three previous accidents or twelve speeding violations or a 1999 speech to the state legislature in which he said, "Bill Janklow speeds when he drives—shouldn't, but he does. When he gets the ticket he pays it." Janklow was sentenced to one hundred days in jail. The family of the slain motorcyclist was unable to sue Janklow because of a law that protects politicians on official business from being responsible for monetary claims. After Janklow served his time, he got his driver's license back and received early reinstatement of his license to practice law—so he has a license to drive, a law license, and a license to get away from responsibility.

A Minor Election

Sam Juhl of Roland, Iowa, is just like a lot of eighteen-year-olds: he's still in high school, he's finally allowed to vote, he can legally buy cigarettes—and he's recently been elected mayor. Juhl placed his name on the ballot for mayor and ran unopposed. When the votes were tallied in November 2005, Juhl, who always thought he was a diamond in the rough, took over the reigns at city hall. "I think I can give them just a young, more youthful approach to the way things are done," Juhl said. The only drawback was at his inaugural party; the toast to the new mayor wasn't made with champagne, because at eighteen, Mayor Sam Juhl was too young to drink alcohol.

IN OCTOBER 2001, A WISCONSIN ETHICS
BOARD OFFICIAL REPRIMANDED STATE
REPRESENTATIVE TIM HOVEN FOR SELLING
SHIRTS OUT OF HIS OFFICE—THE SHIRTS
WERE EMBROIDERED WITH THE LOGO OF
A PRO-LIQUOR LOBBY GROUP.

What's Brown and Sounds Like a Bell?

Florida State Representative Nancy Argenziano was upset when a nursing-home-protection bill for which she had fought was significantly altered, thanks to the help of a notoriously antagonistic industry lobbyist. She became furious when the lobbyist, Jodi Chase, barged into her office, plopped down on her couch, put up her feet, and watched the debate on Argenziano's television. Argenziano wanted to express her anger at the Associated Industries of Florida's lobbyist and decided to send her a pie—a cow pie. So on May 2, 2001, Argenziano lovingly gift-wrapped a twenty-five-pound box of cow manure and sent it to Chase. No matter what people think about Argenziano's gift, the one thing they can't say is she didn't give a sh–t.

Eternal Sunshine of the Spotless Mind

★ ★ ★

Taxpayers in Toronto, Canada, were happy to hear the mayor and the city council promise to be more "transparent" than their predecessors, but soon the meaning of "transparent" would become less than crystal clear. It came out that the council had secretly voted themselves a 12.25 percent pay raise over the next four years; what made matters worse was that the November 2005 pay raise was retroactive to the beginning of the year. Asked by angry constituents how they could claim greater transparency and then secretly raise their own pay, the politicians explained that their raise had been "buried in a confidential report on salary increases for non-union staff" and they simply "don't remember" voting for the raise. I feel better about American politicians now, don't you?

"We have a lot of kids who don't know what 'work' means.
They think 'work' is a four-letter word."

—Senator Hillary Clinton (D-N.Y.), speaking to the
U.S. Chamber of Commerce, May 13, 2006

The Race Is On

In March 2002, Idaho State Representative Kent Higgins (R-Idaho Falls) presented an "award" in the form of a photograph to two colleagues who are advocates of early-childhood education. The recipients of the award were shocked to receive the 1940s-era portrait of beautiful blond-haired, blue-eyed children. Why? Because the children were Nazi *Lebensborn* children—racially pure children created by using eugenics or selective breeding and usually referred to as Ayran children. The frame of the photo was adorned with swastikas. Higgins gave the award because of the legislators' support of a bill to develop preschool programs for four-year-olds. Perhaps Higgins's defense was that no one should have gotten their underwear tied up in little Nazis, as it was all a joke.

"He leads in a way that the good Lord tells him
is best for our country."

—Marine General Peter Pace, chairman of the Joint Chiefs of Staff, on
Defense Secretary Donald Rumsfeld, October 19, 2006

133

Egg on Their Face

★ ★ ★

"**A**s government, we have a different responsibility about advancing the cause of religion, which we are not going to do," said St. Paul, Minnesota, City Council President Kathy Lantry on March 24, 2006. She was referring to a move by the city human rights director, Tyrone Terrill, who'd asked that a cloth Easter bunny, pastel-colored eggs, and a "Happy Easter" sign be removed from city hall, even though no one had complained, because they "could be offensive to non-Christians." My question is, If they're so concerned with not offending other religions, when are they going to change the name of their city—St. Paul?

"If you are not electing Christians, then in essence, you are going to legislate sin."

—Representative Katherine Harris (R-Fla.) in an interview in the *Florida Baptist Witness*, August 24, 2006

A Charming Repartee

★ ★ ★

Shirley Martin, a West Orange, Texas, school board member, was convicted on February 24, 2005, and made to pay a $450 fine after a six-person jury found her guilty of disorderly conduct and assault by threat. The incident in question occured during a closed session of the school board on November 29, 2004, when Martin, a trustee for six years, began a tirade of cursing and was ruled out of order. She continued her "rant," and when fellow trustee Beth Wheeler tried to take control of the situation, Martin threatened Wheeler, saying that if Wheeler interrupted her again, "I'm going to stomp a mud hole in your ass."

"I tell you honestly, I just wanted to stroke him like a kitten and it came out in this gesture. There is nothing behind it."

—Russian President Vladimir Putin, on why he kissed a little boy
on the stomach, July 6, 2006

Macaca Su Caca

★ ★ ★

At a campaign rally in southwest Virginia on August 11, 2006, Senator George Allen (R-Va.) told the crowd he was "going to run this campaign on positive, constructive ideas." He then pointed at S. R. Sidarth, a twenty-year-old Virginian native of Indian descent, saying, "This fellow here, over here with the yellow shirt, Macaca, or whatever his name is. He's with my opponent. . . . Let's give a welcome to Macaca, here." Allen said he didn't know what the word "macaca" meant but thought it sounded like "Mohawk," which he claimed his staff called Sidarth because of his haircut. (Sidarth has a mullet, not a mohawk.) The word "macaca," depending on how you spell it, is either a monkey indigenous to Asia, a town in South Africa, or a racial slur against African immigrants. Allen apologized the following week.

The Fantastic Four

Four out of five isn't bad, unless you're talking about corrupt commissioners. Then it's simply embarrassing. In April 2002 four commissioners in Pensacola, Florida, were indicted for land-sales corruption, and since there really is no honor among thieves, by September two had agreed to testify against a third (the purported leader of the scheme, C. D. Childers). The four Hucksteteers included:

 The owner of a funeral home with a drive-through window who accepted bedroom furniture as a bribe and presented it to his mistress, who rejected it as too cheap.

 Another who took bribe money to buy his daughter-in-law breast implants because she said she was "tired of wearing a training bra."

 Two who claimed their private sessions to discuss their illegal scheme didn't violate the state's open-meetings law because one of them always remained quiet.

Hopefully this Fab Four will be behind bars for at least four seasons.

Sightless Sights Are a Sight

Texas State Representative Edmund Kuempel (R-Seguin) is a proponent of the visually impaired and has submitted a law for the 2007 legislative session that would open up a whole new world for the blind—the world of hunting. Kuempel's bill would allow only legally blind people to use laser sights, spotlights, headlights, or any lighted pointing instruments for hunting; all of which are currently illegal in Texas for sighted people. If passed, this bill would bring a whole different meaning to the phrase "a shot in the dark."

"For the life of me I cannot understand why the terrorists have not attacked our food supply because it is so easy to do."

—Health and Human Services Secretary Tommy Thompson, at a news conference on December 3, 2004, announcing his resignation

A Political Icon

In a *Time* magazine interview (April 3, 2006), former House Majority Leader Tom Delay (R-Tex.), explained the divine intervention behind the infamous mug shot taken during his arrest: "I said a little prayer before I actually did the fingerprint thing, and the picture. And my prayer was basically: 'Let people see Christ through me. And let me smile.' Now, when they took the shot, from my side, I thought it was the fakest smile I'd ever given. But through the camera, it was glowing. I mean, it had the right impact."

This statement gives the impression that DeLay wanted people to see, through the photograph, the humility, forgiveness, and generous nature of the Living Christ. But "right impact," he explained in the next sentence, didn't really mean being "right" with the Lord; it meant giving the "left" the middle finger.

"Poor old left couldn't use [the picture] at all. They had all kind of things planned, they'd spent a lot of money. It made me feel kind of good that all those plans went down the toilet."

Wow, from Christ to the toilet in seven sentences—I'm not sure that's what they mean by seven degrees of separation.

Fisticuffs

★ ★ ★

On February 23, 2005, Colorado State Representative Val Vigil (D-Thornton) introduced a bill to "allow the family of a soldier killed in action to use military license plates." The bill was altered in committee, however, so that family members could use special plates but not the same ones as active military members or veterans. Vigil stood on the Colorado house floor and proposed an amendment to correct the oversight. Representative Bill Cadman (R-Denver) shouted out that Vigil's amendment was "garbage," and Vigil shouted back that Cadman was "garbage." Cadman retorted with the pièce de résistance: "If you try that again, I'll ram my fist up your ass."

"YOU BET WE MIGHT HAVE."

—Senator John Kerry (D-Mass.) when asked if he would have gone to war in Iraq if Saddam Hussein had refused to disarm, August 5, 2004

He's Obviously a Girlies' Man

"She's either Puerto Rican, or the same thing as Cuban, I mean they are all very hot. They have the, you know, part of the black blood in them and part of the Latino blood in them that together makes it."

—California Governor Arnold Schwarzenegger on California's only Latina Republican, Assemblywoman Bonnie Garcia, March 3, 2006

"We don't all agree on everything.
I don't agree with myself on everything."

—2008 presidential hopeful Rudy Giuliani, speaking at the Conservative Political Action Conference, March 2, 2007

You Don't Soothsay?

During the opening prayer on September 4, 2001, Georgia State Representative Dorothy Pelote (D-Savannah) mystified her colleagues by saying, "I can communicate with the dead" and adding that she had "seen" Chandra Levy's body lying in a ditch in the woods. Levy was an intern who'd had an affair with Representative Gary Condit. She went missing on May 1, 2001, and was believed to be dead. On May 22, 2002, Levy's body was found in a wooded area of Washington, D.C., and an overjoyed Pelote said since she "saw" Levy's body in a wooded area and her body was discovered in a wooded area, that proves she has "the gift." I wonder if Pelote's "gift" helped her see that people would always consider her a nut?

ACCORDING TO A DECEMBER 12, 1997, ASSOCIATED PRESS ARTICLE, REPRESENTATIVE DOROTHY PELOTE NOTICED THAT GROCERY BAGGERS WOULD "TAKE THEIR FINGERS TO THEIR TONGUE AND USE THE SALIVA TO HELP THEM OPEN THE BAG." SHE SUBMITTED A "SPIT-FREE BAGGING BILL" THAT WOULD REQUIRE GROCERY STORES TO PROVIDE MOISTENED SPONGES FOR BAGGERS.

Robert's Fools of Order

Missouri State Representative Chuck Graham (D-Columbia) was speaking to the legislative body during an orientation session in December 2002 when freshman Representative Cynthia Davis interrupted him on a point of order. Davis noted that since the state's parliamentary procedure required members to be standing in order to speak, Graham, who was sitting, was out of order. Despite Davis's reprimand, Graham remained in his chair. Was he being defiant? No. Graham, a representative since 1996, had been confined to a wheelchair after a devastating car accident twenty-one years before. Graham may be paralyzed, but it was Davis who wound up looking lame.

"All of a sudden, we see riots,
we see protests, we see people
clashing. The next thing we know,
there is injured or there is dead people.
We don't want to get to that extent."

—California Governor Arnold Schwarzenegger, on the dangers posed if
the courts continued to perform gay marriages, which are against existing
state laws, on NBC'S *Meet the Press*, February 22, 2004

Nothing to Cheer About

"It's just too sexually oriented, you know, the way they're shaking their behinds and going on, breaking it down," said Texas State Representative Al Edwards (D-Houston). "[It's] a distraction that results in pregnancies, dropouts, and the contraction of AIDS and herpes." Was Edwards talking about exotic dancers or prostitutes? Nope. "Those majorettes are doing things that are sexual," Edwards complained. So in March 2005, he submitted legislation requiring cheerleading routines to be "family friendly"; schools that break the rules would have their funding cut. I'm sure the cheerleaders responded to Edwards's legislation with, "Give me an 'F.' Give me a 'U.'" Well, you get the idea.

The Legislative Marshmallow Test

★ ★ ★

"It seems a little silly to have an amendment on Fluff, but it's called for by the silliness of schools offering this as a healthy alternative in the first place," said Massachusetts State Senator Jarrett T. Barrios (D-Cambridge). According to a June 19, 2006, *Boston Globe* article, Barrios introduced an amendment to a junk-food bill that would severely limit the use of Marshmallow Fluff (marshmallow spread) after his son was served a Fluffernutter (peanut butter and Marshmallow Fluff) sandwich as a school lunch. But Massachusetts State Representative Kathi-Anne Reinstein thought Barrios was spreading it on too thick and complained, "I'm protective of Fluff; I grew up on it." To show her love of the fluffy stuff, Reinstein filed a bill to make the Fluffernutter the state's official sandwich. And you thought our politicians wasted their time and your money on frivolous legislation.

"We have not failed in Iraq. . . . The president understands that we need to have a way forward in Iraq that is more successful."

—National Security Adviser Stephen Hadley, December 4, 2006

Not Chuck Wagon but Tongue Waggin'

Sometimes the good-natured ribbing that goes on in a state senate can get out of hand, as it did in March 2005 when Texas State Senator Kel Seliger (R-Amarillo) opened the debate on his resolution officially designating the chuck wagon as the official state vehicle. "Should we call it the Charles wagon?" shouted one senator. "Why not call it the Carlos wagon," said another. When yet another senator asked if he would answer a question, Seliger shot back, "I've already yielded more than a cheerleader at a drive-in." The senate chambers became so quiet you could hear an intern drop. Seliger jokingly said his remark was due to complications from "incipient Tourette's syndrome." Then, as a second thought, he openly remarked, "I think the next bill I do will be for motherhood."

ON JUNE 21, 2005, AFTER AN INTERVIEW WAS OVER, TEXAS GOVERNOR RICK PERRY, BELIEVING THE MICROPHONE AND CAMERA WERE OFF, MOCKED THE FINAL STATEMENT OF THE REPORTER AND ADDED, "ADIOS, MOFO."

This Little Piggy Went to Market

★ ★ ★

When Representative Don Young (R-Alaska) was asked by reporters on September 19, 2005, why he didn't divert funds from his infamous "Bridge to Nowhere" and use the money to help ease the suffering in New Orleans after Hurricane Katrina, he yelled back, "They can kiss my ear! That is the dumbest thing I've ever heard." The "Bridge to Nowhere" (which has already cost taxpayers $223 million) is larger than the Brooklyn Bridge, almost as long as the Golden Gate, and will connect a town of 8,900 people to a town of 50 people. When told by a *New York Times* reporter that another congressman had outspent him in pork projects, Young replied, "I'd like to be a little oinker, myself. If he's the chief porker, I'm upset." He's the one who called himself a pig—not me.

Representative Young has also earmarked $200 million for another "bridge to nowhere"; this one will connect Anchorage to a town with one tenant and a handful of houses.

Newton's Third Law

Tennessee State Representative Chris Newton (R-Cleveland) pleaded guilty on August 30, 2005, to federal charges of bribery and extortion in a government sting called Tennessee Waltz. Newton faces up to twenty-five years in prison for agreeing to sponsor a bill for a fictitious company in exchange for a $3,500 payment. Newton was one of five current or former state lawmakers arrested in the May 2005 sting. Newton said he would stay in the legislature until November and continue to draw full pay and benefits. This reminds me of a classic science experiment on collision: five balls of equal mass hang on five strings, making a horizontal line. One ball is pulled back and released; the ball at the other end bounces off as energy is transferred through the middle balls. The name of the experiment? Newton's balls.

Feelings . . . Nothing More Than Feelings

A memo from the members of the South Carolina legislature's Men's Caucus surfaced in 2001; it advised female pages to wear skimpy clothes and short skirts with underwear optional. All 124 members were requested to attend a two-hour seminar on gender, racial, and ethnic sensitivity scheduled for the start of the 2002 session. Many of the house members turned a cold shoulder to the sensitivity training, including Republican John Graham Altman from Charleston, who said, "I won't be able to attend. I forgot to pack a dress." Altman is not only insensitive, he's also insensible.

"If I see someone come in that's got a diaper on his head and a fan belt wrapped around the diaper on his head, that guy needs to be pulled over."

—Representative John Cooksey (R-La.) during a post-9/11 radio interview; the *Washington Post*, September 20, 2001

Ebony and Ivory

On April 7, 2003, Representative Barbara Cubin (R-Wyo.), debating a gun-control bill on the House floor, commented, "My sons are twenty-five and thirty. They are blond-haired and blue-eyed. One amendment today said we could not sell guns to anybody under drug treatment. So does that mean if you go into a black community, you cannot sell a gun to any black person?" Representative Melvin Watt (D-N.C.), who is black, interrupted Cubin and demanded that she retract the statement. Cubin, who was a little red in the face (and in the neck), claimed she did not mean to offend her "neighbors" on the Democratic side and insisted that her comment was within House rules. I don't know if someone like Cubin is racially insensitive or if she's just being a wise-cracker.

"That's right, I said I'm a hooker. I have to go up to total strangers, ask them for money, and get them to expect me to be there when they need me. What does that sound like to you?"

—Representative Ginny Brown-Waite (R-Fla.), explaining her job description at the Women Impacting Public Policy conference; the *Hill*, October 4, 2005

We Mean No Harm to Your Planet

★ ★ ★

New Mexico State Representative Dan Foley proposed legislation on March 10, 2003, to create a special day to honor aliens. I'm not talking about illegal aliens or legal aliens or even human aliens—I mean aliens that are out of this world. Foley said he would like "Extraterrestrial Culture Day" to commemorate "the many visitations, sightings, unexplained mysteries and technological advances . . . of alien beings." Foley's district is Roswell, New Mexico, the site where some say aliens crash-landed in 1947, and his legislation would "enhance relationships among all the citizens of the cosmos, known and unknown." Foley was so excited after his proposal won approval in the House, he had to "phone home."

★★★★★★★★★

"THE PUBLIC DOESN'T CARE ABOUT FACTS AND FIGURES."

—California gubernatorial candidate Arnold Schwarzenegger, to a gathering of several hundred reporters after the inaugural meeting of his Economic Recovery Council, August 20, 2003

An Alien Concept

While a New Mexico representative is building a bridge to reach out to aliens (see previous story), a representative from Iowa is proposing to build a wall of separation. "I also say we need to do a few other things on top of that wall, and one of them being to put a little bit of wire on top here to provide a disincentive for people to climb over the top or put a ladder there. We could also electrify this wire with the kind of current that would not kill somebody, but it would simply be a discouragement for them to be fooling around with it. We do that with livestock all the time." —Representative Steve King (R-Iowa) showing a scale model of a twelve-foot concrete wall topped with an electrified fence he proposes to run two thousand miles along the border of the United States and Mexico, July 11, 2006

"I don't believe there's any issue that's more important than this one."

—Senator David Vitter (R-La.) discussing not the war in Iraq, the national debt, or our inferior schools but the ultimately failed constitutional amendment banning gay marriage, June 7, 2006

No, Not Hershey, Pennsylvania

"We ask black people: It's time. It's time for us to come together. It's time for us to rebuild a New Orleans, the one that should be a chocolate New Orleans. And I don't care what people are saying in Uptown or wherever they are. This city will be chocolate at the end of the day."

—New Orleans Mayor Ray Nagin promising that blacks, displaced by Hurricane Katrina, will return to the city, at a January 16, 2006, march honoring Dr. Martin Luther King Jr.

"We finally cleaned up public housing in New Orleans. We couldn't do it, but God did."

—Representative Richard Baker (R-La.) to lobbyists, as quoted in the *Wall Street Journal*, September 9, 2005

Road Rules

In the early hours of March 3, 2004, New Mexico House Minority Whip Joe Thompson (R-Albuquerque) was pulled over for erratic driving and given a Breathalyzer test. He blew it; his blood alcohol level was at .12, well above the legal threshold of .08. "While I am terribly embarrassed by this situation, I am thankful that no one else was involved," Thompson said. The irony of this situation is that several hours earlier, Thompson had been at a bill-signing ceremony for legislation he'd spearheaded—calling for tougher penalties for drunk driving. What would have been great is if, when asked about his new drinking bill, Thompson answered, "I thought I paid that."

Child Support

★ ★ ★

"Well, I'll take your questions. . . . I'm not going to ask any of my supporters to leave."

—Representative Tom Reynolds (R-N.Y.), chairman of the House Republican Campaign Committee, surrounded by a group of small children, to a reporter who asked if the children could leave so they could discuss the sexually charged Mark Foley scandal

★★★★★★★★★★

"I AM THE FEDERAL GOVERNMENT."

—Tom DeLay (R-Tex.), to the owner of Ruth's Chris Steak House, after being told to put out his cigar because federal regulations banned smoking in the building, May 14, 2003

What We've Got Here Is a Failure to Communicate

We've all heard the claim that Congress is out of touch with reality. Even if I wanted to disprove this statement, it would be technically impossible with evidence like this. "The Internet is not something you just dump something on. It's not a truck. It's a series of tubes. And if you don't understand, those tubes can be filled and if they are filled, when you put your message in, it gets in line and it's going to be delayed by anyone that puts into that tube enormous amounts of material." —Senate Commerce Committee Chairman Ted Steven (R-Alaska), who is in charge of regulating the Internet, explaining how that dang-fool Internet really works, during a congressional debate, June 28, 2006

"DON'T YOU KNOW WHO I AM?
I'M CONGRESSWOMAN SHEILA JACKSON-
LEE. WHERE IS MY SEAFOOD MEAL?"
DEMANDED SHEILA JACKSON-LEE (D-TEX.)
OF A CONTINENTAL AIRLINES STEWARDESS
IN FEBRUARY 1998. JACKSON-LEE LATER
CALLED THE AIRLINE TO COMPLAIN; THE AGENT
SUGGESTED THAT NEXT TIME SHE FLY DELTA.

The Amazing Rubber Man

New Hampshire State Representative John Kerns (R-New Bedford) was accused of ethics violations in 2004 for bouncing bad checks and threatening a business owner if the man complained. The twenty-three-year-old Kerns also bounced a $3,995 check that had "Honorable John E. Kerns" and "State of New Hampshire" printed on the face—but the check was from his own personal account. At his February 11, 2004, hearing Kerns appeared wearing a black cape he claimed was part of a Knights of Columbus outfit—an organization of which he is a former member. Kerns says he suffers from a recently diagnosed neurological illness that "explains any and all seemingly bizarre behavior . . . [including] my inability to manage my personal finances," but he never submitted proof or identified the diagnosis. He officially bounced himself out of office on February 19, 2004.

ON FEBRUARY 11, 2004, JOHN "THE CAPED CRUSADER" KERNS, WHO IS ALSO A STUDENT AT THE UNIVERSITY OF NEW HAMPSHIRE, "WAS ACCUSED OF USING HIS POSITION AS A LEGISLATOR TO THREATEN OR INTIMIDATE OTHERS." APPARENTLY KERNS FELT HE WAS ENTITLED TO A PARKING SPACE RESERVED FOR SCHOOL OFFICIALS BECAUSE HE'S A STATE LEGISLATOR AND BECAUSE OF THE AFOREMENTIONED ILLNESS.

Not by the Hair on My Chinny Chin Chin

On May 27, 2004, the day after the South Carolina House of Representatives overrode 105 out of 106 budget vetoes by Governor Mark Sanford, he visited the state house with a couple of pigs. By pigs I don't mean police officers; I mean real pigs or, in this case, two piglets—one named "Pork" and the other named "Barrel." "There was a lot of pork-eating yesterday," said Sanford, juggling the squirming pigs. But not everyone was squealing with delight at the governor's ham-handed approach. "This is the people's house," said House Speaker David Wilkins. "I think he defiled it in order to get TV coverage." But what really got defiled was the governor, when the two little piggies went wee-wee-wee (and poop-poop-poop) all over his suit and shoes.

Holy Cow!

★ ★ ★

A half-ton cow nicknamed Moosama bin Laden jumped a six-foot slaughterhouse fence in February 2002 and was on the lam for twelve days before she was finally captured. Cincinnati Mayor Charlie Luken was so impressed by the cow's ability to escape capture that during a special ceremony on April 1, 2002, he presented her with a key to the city. The cow was well behaved until she heard that everyone wanted to have her at the big celebratory barbeque.

"I mean, you got the first mainstream African-American who is articulate and bright and clean and a nice-looking guy. I mean, that's a storybook, man."

—presidential hopeful Joe Biden (D-Del.), on presidential hopeful Barack Obama (D-Ill.) from an interview with the *New York Observer*, February 5, 2007

Knockin' on Heaven's Door

"What occurred to me that morning is something that I imagine a lot of you have thought about, and he's probably figured it out by now. There probably are not seventy-two virgins in the hell he's at and if there are, they probably all look like Helen Thomas," said Representative Steve King (R-Iowa), at the Iowa State Republican Convention, discussing the death of terrorist leader Abu Musab al-Zarqawi on June 17, 2006. (Helen Thomas is an eighty-seven-year-old veteran White House correspondent.)

"If there's one thing that George Bush has done that we should never forget, it's that for us and for our children, he has shattered the myth of white supremacy once and for all."

—Representative Charlie Rangel's (D-N.Y.) closing remarks during a Congressional Black Caucus town hall meeting, September 22, 2005

An Unbalanced Administration

Before Cleveland Mayor Michael R. White left office in January 2002, he told reporters the city was on "solid financial footing" with an $11.8 million surplus. However, when the new mayor, Jane Campbell, took control she was shocked to discover that White's finance director, Kelly Clark, had never really balanced the city's books. When Campbell's new team confronted Clark, she claimed she couldn't remember how she came up with the surplus figure—which, it turned out, was actually a $900,000 deficit. According to one of Campbell's team, Clark confessed that she was unaware that reconciling the books was a prerequisite to declaring a surplus. I wonder if Clark thought that since the word "surplus" has the word "plus" in it, you just have to add everything up to get the balance.

Haines His Way

Perennial presidential candidate Robert Haines (1992, 1996, 2004) was arrested in Fredericksburg, Virginia, in April 2004 for threatening to kill a police officer and his canine partner. According to a police spokesman, Officer Brian Bettis approached Haines when he was handing out flyers and informed him that his car had been parked for four hours in a two-hour zone, and he was going to get a ticket. Bettis reported that Haines then took off his coat and cowboy hat, put his fists up, and told Bettis he was going to "kick his ass and cut off his dog's head." Bettis responded by promptly squirting Haines in the face with pepper spray and arresting him.

ON DECEMBER 1, 1995, ROBERT HAINES WAS CONVICTED OF FELONIOUS RECKLESS CONDUCT AND FELONIOUS USE OF BODY ARMOR AFTER AN ALTERCATION AT THE SALTY DOG BAR IN FEBRUARY OF THAT YEAR. DURING THE TRIAL, HAINES SAID HE WAS WEARING PROTECTIVE BODY ARMOR BECAUSE HE WAS A CANDIDATE FOR THE OFFICE OF U.S. PRESIDENT.

Hassle the Tassel

The city council of San Antonio, Texas, approved an ordinance in December 2004 requiring strippers to wear permits while they are onstage. City Councilman Chip Haass was the mover and shaker behind the $50 "license to thrill" and said he thrust the measure forward to keep dancers from giving a false name if they do something illegal. But in a follow-up report nine months later, Haass admitted there was a bump and grind in the road—only one stripper so far had applied for the license.

"Sometimes, based on the votes that get cast, you wonder whether they're more interested in the rights of the terrorists than in protecting the American people."

—House Majority Leader John Boehner (R-Ohio) on the Democrats in Congress, September 12, 2006

A Real Whiz-bang Politician

During the 2004 presidential campaign, Howard Dean stopped off at the Longfellow Middle School in La Crosse, Wisconsin, and discussed with an eighth-grade science class one of the most important issues of the day: what issues from a canine.

HOWARD DEAN: "Now that we're on dog pee, we can have an interesting conversation about that. . . . Which has more bacteria, dog pee or river water?"

CLASS: Dog pee!

HOWARD DEAN: "I do not recommend drinking urine, but if you drink water straight from the river you have a greater chance of getting an infection than if you drink urine. . . . Now, there are chemicals in urine, waste chemicals that the human body doesn't need, but unless you have an infection, urine is cleaner."

Before leaving, Dean begged the students not to tell their parents that "Howard Dean came to my classroom and advised us to drink water from toilets."

I Said She Was a Cunning Linguist

In the February 23, 2005, edition of the *American Prospect*, Representative Tom Coburn (R-Okla.), claimed that the small town of Coalgate, Oklahoma was overrun with the inhabitants from the isle of Lesbos. "Lesbianism is so rampant in some of the schools in southeast Oklahoma that they'll only let one girl go to the bathroom," he said. I'm sure Coburn meant they only let one girl go to the bathroom at a time; otherwise there would be a whole different type of crisis. However, according to the most recent figures, there are only 234 students at Coalgate High School, and less than half of them are girls. So it's doubtful that much of anything can really be said to be "rampant." The only thing that I see that's rampant is Coburn's fantasy about lesbians in the bathroom.

A Rumble Seat

Supporters of Stephanie Studebaker's race for U.S. House in Ohio were troubled when they logged on to her Web site and read that she had suspended all campaign activities because of "personal issues." The "personal issues" occurred on Sunday, August 13, 2006, when both she and her husband, Sam, were arrested in their home, charged with domestic violence, and booked into the Montgomery County Jail in Dayton. Studebaker decided to put the brakes on her campaign and steer clear of her husband for a while, too.

"This is a great place. Everybody who has announced here has been successful . . . but I have to say that I've already committed to the Food Network to announce."

—2008 presidential hopeful Senator Barack Obama (D-Ill.),
to Jay Leno on *The Tonight Show with Jay Leno*, December 1, 2006

Beleaguered Nations

The La Verkin, Utah, city council passed an anti–United Nations ordinance in July 2001 that prohibits the municipal government from recognizing any U.N. activities and bans flying the U.N. flag at city hall. Proving that some Americans still have the "Don't Tread on Me" mentality, the city received inquiries from across the United States about how to become honorary citizens. The city council quickly came up with the idea of selling certificates of citizenship for $10 each. The money raised went to pay legal expenses caused by the new legislation. It seems to me what the town of La Verkin needed was an anti-lawyer referendum.

A Doggone Good Law

Bob Schwartz, crime adviser for New Mexico's Governor Bill Richardson, was instrumental in getting a law passed during the 2005 legislative session that would really take a bite out of crime. The law would allow felony charges to be filed against owners of "dangerous or potentially dangerous" dogs who have seriously injured or killed another animal or person. On October 16, 2005, not long after the law went into effect, Schwartz was admitted to a hospital suffering from bites on both arms after a dog attacked him. The owner of the dog doesn't have a chance of being prosecuted under the new law—because the dog belong to Schwartz himself.

"THERE'S NOT ANY ONE OF THE CANDIDATES WHO WOULD ARGUE [THAT] THIS DISTRICT IS IN TROUBLE," SAID MICHEAL OCELLO DURING HIS SUCCESSFUL 2006 RUN FOR SCHOOL BOARD IN MEHLVILLE, MISSOURI. IN ADDITION TO BEING ON THE SCHOOL BOARD, MR. OCELLO IS THE BOARD PRESIDENT OF THE ASSOCIATION OF CLUB EXECUTIVES, WHICH REPRESENTS SIX HUNDRED STRIP CLUBS.

What Happens in Vegas Stays in Vegas!

Darlene Heatherington was a well-respected city councilwoman in Lethbridge, Alberta, Canada, but in May 2003 her constituents felt something was missing. They were right, and it turned out to be Heatherington herself. During a trip to Great Falls, Montana, on city business Heatherington went missing. She turned up three days later in Las Vegas and claimed to have been drugged, kidnapped, and sexually assaulted. However, police in Las Vegas, Great Falls, and Lethbridge found serious conflicting elements in her story, and she was charged with filing a false report. It's still a mystery where Heatherington was and what she was doing for those three days. But now everyone knows one place Heatherington is not: sitting on the city council.

"My Fox guys, I love every single one of them."

—Secretary of State Condoleezza Rice, caught on an open mike between morning interviews, stating her preference for the right-leaning Fox News correspondents, January 11, 2007

Sauron Santorum

To show that he's got a solid and realistic grasp on the situation in Iraq, Senator Rick Santorum (R-Pa.) told a reporter from the *Bucks County Courier Times* on October 17, 2006, "As the hobbits are going up Mount Doom, the Eye of Mordor is being drawn somewhere else." (The Eye of Mordor was how the evil Lord Sauron searched for the Ring that would consolidate his power over Middle-earth.) "It's being drawn to Iraq and it's not being drawn to the U.S. You know what? I want to keep it on Iraq. I don't want the Eye to come back here to the United States." I'll bet Santorum now wishes he had said "precious" little.

In an attempt at a filibuster to hinder voting on legislation, on January 8, 2005, Colorado State Senator Tom Wiens (R-Castle Rock) attempted to speak extemporaneously for twenty-four consecutive hours. He reached hour sixteen before realizing it was Saturday.

Illegal Aliens Illegal

★ ★ ★

Florida State Senator Frederica Wilson (D-Miami) wants to completely ban aliens—not the people or even little green men, but just the word. "I personally find the word 'alien' offensive when applied to individuals, especially to children," said Wilson in an interview on February 27, 2007. "An alien to me is someone from out of space." So she introduced legislation (SB 2154) that reads in part, "A state agency or official may not use the term 'illegal alien' in an official document of the state." Asked what word she would prefer over "alien," Wilson said, " 'Illegal' I can live with, but I like 'undocumented' better." Her legislation, however, is forthright with no bite—there is no penalty for using the words.

Looking for a Few Good Men

★ ★ ★

"I'm just looking to get together with any white guy who's got a great body on him, a good size endowment that's cut, just get together, get naked, play with one another, get each other off. Nothing hard-core. I have to be incredibly careful, incredibly safe, incredibly discreet. I can't overemphasize that," said Representative Edward Schrock (R-Va.) in a recording on a gay-sex personals phone line. Schrock dropped his bid for reelection on August 30, 2004, after Michael Rogers on blogACTIVE.com, reported that Schrock is gay.

"GOD IS THE ONE WHO CHOOSES OUR RULERS."

—Representative Katherine Harris (R-Fla.) in an interview in the *Florida Baptist Witness* on August 24, 2006, explaining why the separation of church and state is "a lie"

An Embarrassing Track Record

Racing legends Richard Petty and Darrell Waltrip and their supporters visited Washington State lawmakers to request that a racetrack be built in the Evergreen State. They were met with less than open arms and a lot of narrow-mindedness. On February 21, 2007, Representative Larry Seaquist (D-Gig Harbor) told the *Seattle Times* his opinion of NASCAR fans: "These people are not the kind of people you would want living next door to you. They'd be the ones with the junky cars in the front yard and would try to slip around the law." Speaker of the House Frank Chopp said of seven-time NASCAR champion Richard Petty, "I was going to make a bad joke about, 'Who's he.' But then I decided, 'You mean the guy who got picked up for DUI, that guy?'" Petty, however, has no record of any alcohol-related issues. In fact, he's famous for, throughout his career, refusing alcohol advertising on any of his cars. Looks like Chopp is guilty of another form of DWI: Dissing Without Information.

Earth to Mr. Davis, Earth to Mr. Davis

"My vision is to make the most diverse state on earth, and we have people from every planet on the earth in this state. We have the sons and daughters of every, of people from every planet, of every country on earth."

—former California Governor Gray Davis,
hoping to avoid a recall vote, September 17, 2003

Texas Governor Rick Perry told an audience in the city of Midland he was glad to be in Abilene to start his 2006 reelection campaign.

Sock It to Me!

★ ★ ★

"If one person criticizes our sheriffs or says one more thing [about the local authorities' Hurricane Katrina and Rita relief efforts], including the president of the United States, he will hear from me. One more word about it after this show airs, and I . . . might likely have to punch him, literally," announced Senator Mary Landrieu (D-La.) on *This Week with George Stephanopoulous* on September 4, 2005. Even though it is a federal offense to threaten the president, no action was taken against Landrieu. Probably because the Bush administration had already hit an all-time low and didn't need another black eye.

"Isn't that the ultimate homeland security, standing up and defending marriage?"

—Senator Rick Santorum (R-Pa.) on the Senate floor, regarding the failed constitutional amendment banning gay marriage, July 14, 2004

The Tar Baby Chronicles, Part I

The term "tar baby" is a metaphor for any "sticky situation" that is only made worse by efforts to escape it. Originally from an Uncle Remus story about a human figure made of tar used as a trap by Brer Fox to capture Brer Rabbit, the term is now identified more as a derogatory phrase about African-Americans, and using it at all is a tar baby in itself. But these politicians just seem to grin and brer it.

 "The best thing politically would be to stay as far away from that tar baby as I can."

> —Massachusetts Governor and potential 2008 presidential candidate Mitt Romney, on Boston's troubled highway tunnel project called the Big Dig, in Ames, Iowa, July 29, 2006

 "Having said that, I don't want to hug the tar baby of trying to comment on the program—the alleged program—the existence of which I can neither confirm nor deny."

> —White House Press Secretary Tony Snow during a May 16, 2006, press briefing on Bush's questionable surveillance program

The Tar Baby Chronicles, Part II

 "For me to stand here and . . . say I'm going to declare divorces invalid because of someone who feels they weren't treated fairly in court, we are getting into a tar baby of enormous proportions and I don't know how you get out of that."

—2008 presidential hopeful Senator John McCain (R-Ariz.) at a town hall meeting in Cedar Falls, Iowa, March 16, 2007

 "Everybody on my staff, everybody I knew thought I was crazy, and said, 'Don't do this.' They said it's a no-win tar baby."

—Senator John Kerry, considering whether to lead a new investigation into the fate of prisoners of war and other Americans who never came home from Vietnam, *New York Times*, August 11, 1992

Looks Like He Needs Regrooving

On the November 2003 ballot in Denver, Colorado, there was a referendum requesting that the city council research various proposals on how to help people relax, take it easy, and just chill out. The "peace initiative" was championed by former Transcendental Meditation teacher Jeff Peckman, who claimed the need for the legislation was because "the buildup of society-wide stress is like a new pollution in the environment." Said Councilman Charlie Brown, "What are we supposed to do, hand out incense sticks at Denver International Airport? Is that the image we want for our city?" Oh, good grief, Charlie Brown, don't be such a blockhead—the voters rejected the ballot initiative by more than a two-to-one margin.

In May 2001, Tye Thomas resigned as mayor of
Gun Barrel City, Texas. A week earlier Thomas had
telephoned the police and begged them to arrest him
because he was intoxicated in public.

Duty, or Doodie, on Your Customs

The small town of Hérouxville, Quebec, has decided to tell immigrants and the rest of the country where it stands on certain issues. In January 2007 the city adopted a declaration of "norms," which stated: It is forbidden to stone women or burn them with acid. Children cannot carry weapons to school (even though the Supreme Court of Canada ruled that members of the Sikh religion can carry a kirpan, a ceremonial dagger, in schools). You can't cover or hide your face at any time, other than on Halloween. Female police officers are allowed to arrest male suspects. And women are allowed to drive, dance, and make decisions on their own. "We're telling people who we are," said André Drouin, a town councillor and the primary force behind the legislation. Actually, what the legislation does is tell some people who they can't be because their customs conflict with the new town laws. Although I think the rule about not stoning women or burning them with acid is a good one, don't you?

D.U.M.B.

★ ★ ★

State Senator Jeff Wentworth and State Representative Ruth McClendon, both of San Antonio, Texas, successfully sponsored a bill in 2005 changing the title of assistant secretary of state to deputy secretary of state because of concerns that the acronym for the assistant secretary of state (ASS) might offend people. I doubt an acronym is going to offend people, but if the assistant secretary of state turns out to be a real ass—they might be offended.

★ ★ ★ ★ ★ ★ ★ ★ ★

"GAY MARRIAGE SHOULD BE BETWEEN A MAN AND A WOMAN."

—California Governor Arnold Schwarzenegger, in a radio interview with Sean Hannity, *New York Daily News*, August 29, 2003

Gift Horse or Gift Whores?

"The City That Cares," Chesapeake, Virginia, tried unsuccessfully for ten years to acquire the domain name Chesapeake.com, which would be simpler than the one it's been using, cityofchesapeake.net. Finally, after being contacted every six months by Public Communications Coordinator Lizz Gunnufsen, Aspen Technology, the owner of the desirable URL, gave the city the domain name for free. "I didn't really ever think we would get it," said Gunnufsen. The city officially acquired the coveted name in October 2005, and in summer 2006 it turned around and sold it to Chesapeake Energy Corporation for $120,000. Because of the way its generosity was taken advantage of, Aspen Technology should rename itself Asburned Technology.

"I MYSELF HAVE EDUCATED MYSELF ABOUT THE SEVERITY OF THE ARTICLES OF IMPEACHMENT, AND I WANT TO SHARE WITH MY COLLEAGUES AND THE AMERICAN PEOPLE SOME OF THE THOUGHTS THAT I HAVE LEARNED."

—Representative Patrick Kennedy (D-RI) during the
1999 Clinton impeachment trial

Couch That Aggression

"It will be educative and address things like literacy, anger management, and provide counseling to give them life skills that will help them overcome these tendencies," said the spokeswoman for Australian Attorney General Philip Ruddock. So who will receive this treatment? Suspected terrorists, that's who. The Australian government announced a rehabilitation program in February 2007 designed to help impressionable would-be terrorists "change the behavior that's resulted in them being the subject of a control order." I wonder if the program will consist of statements like "Now put down that bomb and tell me how you really feel."

"I never know what I'm going to say until I say it, so I am kind of interested in hearing what I think."

—South Carolina Representative John Graham Altman (R-Charleston), during debate on a mandatory-seat-belt provision, April 2003

A Far-Flung Story

She was called "the Wild Woman of Albany," and I'm not talking about some notorious gun-slinging politician from the Wild West—I'm talking about coffee-slinging Ada Smith, a New York State senator from 1988 to 2006. During her career, more than two hundred of her staffers either quit or were fired, mainly because of Smith's infamous temper. On August 26, 2006, Smith was found guilty of harassment, a reduction from the original misdemeanor assault charge, for throwing hot coffee at and pulling a hairpiece off aide Jennifer Jackson's head. But that one incident alone wouldn't earn her the moniker "the Wild Woman of Albany." Here are other things Smith is accused of throwing: a trash can, a desk organizer, stacks of paper, and a melted ice-cream bar. She threatened one staffer with a knife, one with a cleaver, called another "white trash" and "a fag," and was convicted of speeding past a security checkpoint at a state garage in Albany in 2004. So the next time you see your boss, you might just want to say, "Thank you."

IN JULY 1998 ADA SMITH WAS ACCUSED
OF BITING BROOKLYN POLICE OFFICER
SETH KAUFMAN AS HE TRIED TO ARREST HER
FOR INTERFERING WITH POLICE BUSINESS.
THE ALTERCATION AROSE AFTER SMITH
BECAME ANNOYED THAT KAUFMAN'S PATROL
CAR WAS BLOCKING TRAFFIC; HE WAS
QUESTIONING A DRIVER AHEAD OF HER,
AND SHE DEMANDED TO GET BY. SMITH WAS
SPRAYED WITH MACE, HANDCUFFED, AND
CHARGED WITH RESISTING ARREST.

A Real Wing Nut

In February 2003 the national security alert had been elevated to orange, indicating a possible terrorist attack. The residents of Geneseo, Illinois, aware of the heightened alert, were alarmed when an F-15, followed by a smaller airplane, buzzed their town, rattling windows and bringing people out into the streets. It turned out the F-15 was piloted by Major Whitney Sieben of the Oregon Air National Guard, who "wanted to do a flyover for his Grandma Sieben." The smaller airplane was piloted by Sieben's uncle, State Senator Todd Sieben (R-Geneseo). Senator Sieben said he understood the concerns of the townfolk "because of the timing, with the elevated [security] level to orange. I understand why they would think there is something going on." With the threat of a terrorist attack a lot of Americans are living on a wing and a prayer, but with politicians like Sieben, we might not even have a prayer.

Both Had Faulty Internal Structures

★ ★ ★

"I absolutely feel that the same thing that happened at the World Trade Center has hit me. I was terrorized [by the *Frederick News-Post*]."

—outgoing Frederick, Maryland, Mayor Jim Grimes, on November 8, 2001, reacting to a judge's decision to allow an arrested prostitute's file to be publicly disclosed—all the while claiming he was protecting some friends

"IT'S AGAINST THE LAW IN AMERICA TO HIRE PEOPLE ILLEGALLY."

—Senator John Kerry (D-Mass.) during a 2004 presidential debate

Rooster Booster

In 2002 Oklahoma joined forty-seven other states in banning cockfighting, the sport of forcing gamecocks armed with razorlike spurs on their legs to fight each other, usually to the death (or at least until one of them rips out the other one's McNuggets). But in January 2005, Oklahoma State Senator Frank Shurden proposed legislation to bring this glamorous and majestic "sport" back to his state; he said it would create a boon in gambling and tourism. To thwart potential cock-a-doodle-don'ts, Shurden suggested that the roosters wear tiny boxing gloves instead of spurs, along with electronic-sensitive vests to record the number of strikes—thereby taking the blood out of this blood sport. But in April 2004 the cock crowed three times when Shurden's legislation came up for a vote, signifying the three votes that coldcocked the bill's passage.

Boxer Shorts

★ ★ ★

"Greg's naked body was long and elegant, his embrace enveloped her utterly, and they meshed with ease and grace. He smelled good too, faintly and astringently of aftershave. He was clinging to her as if he'd never let her go, it was all so easy and right."

—excerpt from the novel *A Time to Run* by Senator Barbara Boxer (D-Calif.)

"I think incest can be handled as a family matter within the family. The people know about it and they can get more serious about it. But I don't think it's rape because of the awareness of it within the family."

—Republican Jay Dickey (R-Ark.), when he was running for U.S. Congress, at an El Dorado, Arkansas, Rotary Club in July 1992, explaining why he's against the "incest" exception many right-to-lifers make for abortion

Phony Phone Bill

During the November 2000 election cycle, more than three thousand residents in the Phoenix, Arizona, area answered the phone in the middle of the night only to hear an automated campaign pitch for Republican State Senator John Huppenthal. As part of his campaign, Huppenthal had bragged about his instrumental efforts in passing a law banning automated telemarketing calls.

ROBERT MARSHALL, A STAFFORDSHIRE, ENGLAND, COUNTY COUNCILLOR, WAS ALLOWED £10,000 TO SPEND ON ANY PROJECT HE WISHED IN 2003, AND HE USED THE MONEY TO PURCHASE A MOBILE SPEED CAMERA TO CATCH LEAD-FOOTED DRIVERS. A FEW MONTHS LATER, MARSHALL WAS PHOTOGRAPHED BY THE VERY SAME CAMERA GOING FORTY-TWO-MILES-PER-HOUR IN A THIRTY-MILES-PER-HOUR ZONE.

Long-Suffering Cubs Fan

In February 1996 the Oklahoma senate passed a bill that outlawed the increasingly popular but grisly sport of bear wrestling. Not nude "bare wrestling," but an event usually held in bars where participants actually tangle with small declawed bears. If arrested for this unbearable act, a wrestler could be fined as much as $5,000. Senator Penny Williams successfully tagged on an amendment to the bill, albeit unrelated, that raised the fine for spousal abuse, but she could only get the legislation to agree upon a maximum penalty for that crime of $2,000. Injustices like these are common in the world of politics; apparently, we're supposed to just grin and bear it.

Monitoring the Moniter

In July 2005, New York State Assemblyman Willis Stephens apologized to an Internet-based message-board discussion group after inadvertently blasting 285 e-mails—one to every member on the list. Assemblyman Stephens, who is also a practicing attorney, claimed the message was intended to go only to an aide and said that he doesn't routinely "post messages" himself; apparently he likes to simply eavesdrop. Group member Peter Hansen strongly objected to the sentence "watching the idiots pontificate" used in Stephens's e-mail, because "pontificating idiots" is an oxymoron, he fired back, "sort of like an honest politician or an ethical attorney." Another reason why it's a good idea to have a "Do you want to send mail now?" prompt on your computer.

Not a Suicide Bomber but a Cherry Bomber

★ ★ ★

When running for any political office it's a good idea to do some soul searching and some memory searching as well—especially if you remember that you're wanted by the FBI. Partway through the 2000 race for Scottsdale, Arizona, City Council, Gary Tredway resigned, claiming that he had leukemia. But an article in the *Scottsdale Tribune* told the real story. Tredway's real name is Howard Mechanic (really), and he was arrested the night after the Kent State killings for throwing a cherry bomb during a violent protest. During the May 5, 1970, protest, the ROTC building burned down, and Mechanic and his friend Larry Kogan became the first students charged under President Nixon's Civil Obedience Act of 1968. Mechanic stayed on the lam for thirty years and then decided to run for city council. As one of President Bill Clinton's last acts, on January 20, 2001, his last day in office, he granted Mechanic a presidential pardon. We've all heard that Bill Clinton said he never inhaled, but I bet Mechanic gave out a huge exhalation after everything was over.

Have a Nice Trip

The Bristol, England, City Council is cracking down on hazardous conditions and demanding that all hazmats be removed. The hazmats I'm referring to aren't hazardous materials but hazardous mats—doormats. The council issued a letter to thiry-two thousand tenants demanding removal of all doormats by September 18, 2006, as they pose a "tripping risk." Ted Marshall, chairman of the Brookridge House tenants' association, in Henbury, said, "These people must be sitting in offices with nothing better to do." Offices, I'm sure, that have a nice welcome mat at the front door.

A bill was introduced in the
New Hampshire legislature that
would make it legal to use and sell
marijuana. The bill was sponsored
by the representative from Keene,
New Hampshire: Charles Weed.

Up, Up, and Away

★ ★ ★

"Go balloons! Go balloons! Go balloons! I don't see anything happening. . . . Jesus! We need more balloons. I want all balloons to go, goddammit. . . . There's not enough coming down! All balloons, what the hell! There's nothing falling! What the f—k are you guys doing up there?"

—Don Mischer, producer of the July 30, 2004,
Democratic National Convention in Boston's Fleet Center, overheard on CNN
after the balloons failed to drop at the end of the ceremony

According to an article in the October 20, 2006, edition of the *St. Louis Post-Dispatch*, the election board of St. Louis County, Missouri, admitted that an unnamed election judge had cast two absentee ballots for the November 7 election. The board, however, shielded the man's actions, claiming he was old and probably simply forgot that he had already voted.

The Final Solution

City officials in Santa Monica, California, announced a really squirrelly plan in 2005 that made it unnecessary for male squirrels to hide their nuts anymore. The city administered birth-control shots to the city's squirrels using GonaCon, a serum that halts ovulation in female squirrels and testicular development in males. The makers of the drug say the shot does not have any dangerous side effects, but apparently no one asked the squirrels about that. Researchers say the shot takes about three months to take effect. I wonder if any moral conservatives protested the inoculations on the grounds that it would promote promiscuity among the sterile squirrel community.

IN JUNE 1995 CHRISTINE WALKER AND
JEREMY BUCKELS WERE FOUND BY POLICE IN
A COUNCIL BLUFFS, IOWA, CITY PARK AFTER
ITS TEN P.M. CLOSING. THEY AGREED TO PAY A
FINE, BUT WALKER FEARED A "TRESPASSING"
CONVICTION ON HER RECORD AND ASKED THE
PROSECUTOR TO RECONSIDER. AFTER SOME
DELIBERATION, THE PROSECUTOR HAD THE
CONVICTION CHANGED TO A VIOLATION OF THE
1975 CITY ORDINANCE MAKING IT ILLEGAL
"TO WORRY" BLACK SQUIRRELS.

A Trip and a Fall
★ ★ ★

Florida State Senator Mandy Dawson (D-Fort Lauderdale) felt left out when fellow legislators planned a trip to Africa on their own dime. In an April 12, 2005, letter to lobbyists, Dawson said, "I need to raise funds to help defray the cost. . . . Due to ethics regulations, the check should be made out to the Florida Caucus of Black State Legislators." She obviously knew that what she was doing was unethical and possibly illegal, because she was a member of the Senate Ethics and Election Committee. After being reprimanded in public by the senate, she apologized in a statement that referred to problems she faced as a single mother and as a candidate and mentioned memories of a malnourished puppy she'd had as a child.

In 2002, Florida State Senator Mandy Dawson was arrested for altering a prescription to get extra painkillers. She avoided a prison sentence by agreeing to go into drug rehab.

John . . . I Am Your Father

★ ★ ★

"I'm telling you, they're shooting at me from everywhere. Everybody's against me. Governor Engler, Governor Bush, all the governors, all the senators, but we're going to kill them, right? We're going to get them. I'm getting out of that Death Star, and we're going to win this election."

—Senator John McCain, rallying his troops, or maybe his Clone Troopers or Imperial Stormtroopers, in Michigan during his failed 2000 presidential bid, February 22, 2000

"I feel like Luke Skywalker trying to get out of the Death Star."

—presidential candidate and possible space cadet John McCain, describing his intergalactic battle with his own party concerning campaign finance reform, February 5, 2000

No Room in the Inn

Measure G, or the Transient Occupancy Tax, was placed on the ballot in Cotati, California, for the November 7, 2006, election. The measure simply proposed to raise the hotel tax in town from 10 percent to 12 percent. No big deal, right? According to Fred H. Levin, executive director of the Sonoma County Taxpayers' Association, the problem was that "There are no hotels, motels, inns, or lodges in Cotati." Not to be thwarted by such a silly little fact, Councilwoman Lisa Moore rebutted, "We're being proactive." Town members thought the measure didn't measure up logically, and it was defeated at the polls. This is kind of a perversion of *Field of Dreams*—if you tax it, they will build it.

On September 17, 2001, Senator Hillary Clinton (D-N.Y.) told Jane Pauley on NBC's *Dateline* that her daughter, Chelsea, nearly perished in the World Trade Center collapse. Unbeknownst to her, Chelsea was writing a piece stating that even though she was in Manhattan during the attack she was nowhere near the towers.

Treasurer, Balance Thyself

★ ★ ★

The *Rocky Mountain News* (Colorado) wrote on November 21, 2006, that Doug Milliken, the newly elected Arapahoe County treasurer, was in the process of losing his house due to foreclosure. Milliken's campaign flyers had promised that he would "educate homeowners on how to make wise decisions to avoid losing their homes" and "empower families to save their home when faced with foreclosure." But outgoing Arapahoe County Treasurer Adrian "Bernie" Ciazza said Milliken "won on false pretenses [because] the treasurer has absolutely no ability to help people avoid foreclosure." Milliken's motto must be "Always look on the bright side of life," because he stated that he'll take what he learned from the foreclosure process to help people in similar circumstances. "It's just amazing that I have some personal experience," he said. Like they say, "Teach what you know."

"If I were to lose my mind right now and pick one of you up and bash your head against the floor and kill you, would that be right?"

—presidential candidate Alan Keyes on January 31, 2000, enlightening a class of fifth graders about the morality of abortion

Killing Killers

★ ★ ★

"I favor the death penalty for abortionists and other people who take life," claimed Congressman Tom Coburn (R-Okla.) in an interview with the Associated Press on July 10, 2004. As a doctor, he admitted to having performed two abortions himself (to save the lives of mothers with congenital heart disease) but said he opposes the procedure in cases of rape. This is along the same logical lines as the slogans "Stamp out violence" and "Judgmental people are idiots."

According to an article in the November 7, 2006, *Austin American-Statesman*, former Texas statehouse member Rick Green took a swing at Patrick Rose after Green arrived at a Baptist church polling facility where Rose was greeting voters. Rose was the man who'd taken Green's position after beating him by a few hundred votes in 2002.

Please Remove Price Tag

The Texas Ethics Commission voted five to three in November 2006 that from now on state officials don't have to report how much cash they received as a "gift" but only that they received "currency." In a previous ruling, the commission had decided that two checks for $100,000 could be reported simply as "checks." An astounded Texas district attorney summed it up by saying the decision makes it "perfectly legal to report the gift of 'a wheelbarrow' without reporting that the wheelbarrow was filled with cash." But surely, fair citizens, our elected officials are too forthright to abuse a regulation like this—aren't they?

IN MAY 2006 BOTH THE CONGRESSIONAL OFFICES AND THE HOME OF WILLIAM JEFFERSON (D-LA.) WERE RAIDED BY FBI AGENTS AS PART OF AN ONGOING BRIBERY STING. "THEY FOUND $90,000 OF THE CASH IN THE FREEZER, IN $10,000 INCREMENTS WRAPPED IN ALUMINUM FOIL AND STUFFED INSIDE FROZEN-FOOD CONTAINERS," REPORTED CNN. EVEN HAVING SECRETED ALL THIS COLD, HARD CASH DIDN'T COST JEFFERSON THE ELECTION—HE WAS REELECTED ON DECEMBER 9, 2006.

Booze Blues

★ ★ ★

Teresa L. Kaiser resigned as the executive director of the Oregon Liquor Control Commission on April 27, 2006, "due to," she said, "circumstances that I deeply regret." The circumstances happened five days earlier when Kaiser was arrested after swerving into oncoming traffic, causing an accident and an injury; she subsequently registered double the legal blood alcohol limit. Kaiser confessed to police that she had merely had two glasses of wine over a period of several hours, but according to research released by Kaiser's own agency, in order to achieve a blood alcohol level of 0.16 percent she would have had to have had six drinks in one hour. Again, the name of Kaiser's commission is the Oregon Liquor Control Commission—she got the liquor part right, she just overlooked the control.

"I think everybody can look at my life and what I've done and say that's not true. I mean, she was such a bitch," said Representative Cass Ballenger (R-N.C.), who is white, denying that he is a racist, but confessing to having "segregationist feelings" about former Representative Cynthia McKinney (D-Ga.), who is black, in December 2002.

Dedicated to the One I Love—Me!

★ ★ ★

According to the watchdog organization Citizens Against Government Waste, federal law prohibits the naming of federal structures after sitting members of Congress. Sounds like a simple-to-understand law, but apparently not so to Senator Robert Byrd (D-W.Va.). Here is a partial list of projects earmarked by Byrd—basically signed, sealed, and delivered.

- ✔ Robert C. Byrd Locks and Dam
- ✔ Robert C. Byrd Green Bank Telescope
- ✔ Robert C. Byrd Drive, which runs from Beckley to Sophia (Byrd's hometown)
- ✔ Robert C. Byrd National Technology Transfer Center at Wheeling Jesuit University
- ✔ Robert C. Byrd Highway
- ✔ Robert C. Byrd Federal Correctional Institution
- ✔ Robert C. Byrd High School
- ✔ Robert C. Byrd Freeway

Giving Us the Byrd

★ ★ ★

Here's another flock of Senator Robert Byrd's (D-W.Va.) signature projects:

 Robert C. Byrd Center for Hospitality and Tourism

 Robert C. Byrd Science Center

 Robert C. Byrd Health Sciences Center of West Virginia

 Robert C. Byrd Cancer Research Center

 Robert C. Byrd Technology Center at Alderson-Broaddus College

 Robert C. Byrd Hardwood Technologies Center, near Princeton

 Robert C. Byrd Bridge between Huntington and Chesapeake, Ohio

 Robert C. Byrd addition to the lodge at Oglebay Park, Wheeling

 Robert C. Byrd Community Center, Pine Grove

 Robert C. Byrd Honors Scholarships

 Robert C. Byrd Expressway, U.S. 22 near Weirton

 Robert C. Byrd Institute in Charleston

 Robert C. Byrd Institute for Advanced Flexible Manufacturing

 Robert C. Byrd Visitor Center at Harpers Ferry National Historic Park

 Robert C. Byrd Federal Courthouse

SPEAKER OF THE HOUSE NANCY PELOSI
(D-CALIF.) SECURED $1 MILLION TO FUND THE
MILITARY INTELLIGENCE SERVICE HISTORIC
LEARNING CENTER (BUILDING 640). IN A
SEPTEMBER 29, 2006, PRESS RELEASE,
SHE SAID THE CENTER WILL SERVE AS AN
"EDUCATION CENTER AND PROJECT TO
PRESERVE THE SITE OF THE U.S. ARMY'S
FIRST LANGUAGE SCHOOL ESTABLISHED IN
1941." THE MONEY FOR THIS PROJECT WAS
TAKEN FROM THE FISCAL YEAR 2007
DEFENSE APPROPRIATIONS BILL.

Something's Got His Goat

In September 2002, the San Francisco *Bay Area Reporter* noted that Makinka Moye, who was running for city supervisor, had been arrested earlier that year for beating a goat to death and then butchering its carcass in a vacant lot near a city recreation center. Hey, with so many barbecues that candidates must attend, they've got to get the meat from somewhere, right?

In April 2001, the city council president in
Elizabeth, New Jersey, had a councilman who interrupted her
too often handcuffed and arrested.

I Beg Your Pardon

★ ★ ★

On December 23, 2003, New York Governor George Pataki pardoned a comedian who had been convicted on a misdemeanor charge for performing an "obscene, indecent, immoral, and impure" show at a Manhattan nightclub. Robin Williams, Phyllis Diller, and other entertainers, along with a group of lawyers and writers, had petitioned the governor to pardon the comedian on the grounds that he was simply exercising his right of free speech. The governor agreed and signed the pardon for Lenny Bruce, an infamous ground-breaking comedian, who had died from a heroin overdose thirty-seven years earlier. As Bruce said, "They call it the Halls of Justice because the only place you get justice is in the halls."

"We're not going to tell you what our plan is, Jon, because you're just going to go out and blow it."

—Senator Conrad Burns (R-Mont.) in a debate with
Democrat challenger Jon Tester on why he's not going to divulge
the secret plan he and President Bush have to win the Iraq war;
Billings Gazette, October 18, 2006

Don't Quit Your Day Job

In 2002, Senator Zell Miller (D-Ga.) declared that because "the pickup owners of this nation might get screwed in all this gas-guzzler talk about SUVs and vans," he cowrote, sang, and recorded, "The Talking Pickup Truck Blues." Some of the lyrics to the song go as follows:

> I hear some news from Washington
> Of a crackpot scheme to raise some mon.
> It's an unkind way to raise a buck,
> And it adds more cost to my pickup truck.

And seventy-year-old Senator Barbara Mikulski (D-Md.) publicly sang "Who Let the Dogs Out?"

His Uncles Would Be Proud

After Representative Patrick Kennedy (D-R.I.) was accused of causing $28,000 in damages to a rented yacht during a cruise to celebrate the New Year 2000 (or Y2K), he appeared at a political roast dressed in a sailor suit. In the spirit of the motto of the great seaman Popeye the Sailor, "I am what I am," Kennedy sang the sailing chantey "Patrick the Sailor Man."

During the same event, Kennedy, who admitted to having used cocaine, joked about another coke user, Senator Lincoln Chafee (R-R.I.) by saying, "Now when I hear someone talking about a Rhode Island politician whose father was a senator and who got to Washington on his family name, used cocaine, and wasn't very smart, I know there is only a fifty-fifty chance it's me."

It's a Dog's Life

★ ★ ★

It looks like Kentucky's government has finally gone to the dogs. Abby, a white West Highland terrier belonging to Governor Ernie and Glenna Fletcher, has her own stationery, complete with stamped doggy signature and seasonal cards featuring her photograph, which are handed out at the capitol's front desk. Abby wears bunny ears for Easter, a pumpkin cap for Thanksgiving, and is surrounded by poinsettias for Christmas. According to an October 29, 2006, Associated Press article, Abby also has a page on the governor's mansion's Web site, with a video of her giving a tour. It's no wonder Abby is more popular than the governor, who had a 31 percent approval rating in December 2006. Maybe if he passed out pictures of himself with cute bunny ears he wouldn't be in the political doghouse.

Barbara or Barbarella

★ ★ ★

Barbara Cubin (R-Wyo.) made political news even before she arrived in Congress in 1995. While in the Wyoming state legislature, she passed around penis-shaped cookies to her male colleagues; she told Roll Call in 1994 that she hadn't baked them herself. She later explained this act by saying, "People sometimes do things that they wouldn't do in front of their mother." Then, during the 2000 Florida presidential recount debacle, she screamed in a meeting, "We are bending over and taking it from the Democrats!" When some of her colleagues expressed shock at her rather un-family-values verbiage, she snapped, "Quiet down or you'll get a spanking." Maybe someone should give her a black bustier, knee-high leather boots, and make her the House minority whip.

"It is a better and more important story than losing a couple of soldiers every day."

—Representative George Nethercutt Jr. (R-Wash.), speaking at an October 13, 2003, meeting at the University of Washington's Daniel J. Evans School of Public Affairs, explaining how the rebuilding of Iraq was a better news story than one about American soldiers killed in battle

Like Taking Gandhi from a Baby

While campaigning for Senate candidate Nancy Farmer in St. Louis, Missouri, on January 3, 2004, Senator Hillary Rodham Clinton (D-N.Y.) wanted to end her speech with one of Farmer's favorite quotes from Mahatma Gandhi. For no apparent reason, she blurted, "It's from Mahatma Gandhi, he ran a gas station down in St. Louis for a couple of years. Mr. Gandhi"—she'd pointed at someone in the audience—"do you still go to the gas station? Lot of wisdom comes out of that gas station." Clinton later apologized on CNN, saying, "It was a lame attempt at a joke." In a prepared statement, she tried to explain that she was aiming for a comedic punch line in that certain ethnic groups were associated strongly with operating American gas stations. At least she didn't ask the question, "What's a Hindu?" and then answer, "It lays eggs."

Un Unreasonable Politician

★ ★ ★

During a trial in November 2001, Pennsylvania State Representative Jane Baker told a jury that she "needs help with reading and understanding material and carrying on conversations" after suffering head injuries in a traffic accident. Baker said her cognitive abilities had been so damaged that she is "virtually unemployable" except for her position in the legislature. She promised, however, that in spite of her brain trauma she would run for a second term in 2002. According to the *Allentown Morning Call*, the jury awarded her $2.9 million; I hope it was a bribe not to run.

In 2001, the Texas senate passed a resolution designating the pecan as the official state health nut of Texas.

A Pro-Choice Candidate

"If they want to be a homosexual or bisexual when they turn eighteen that's fine and good. But I think we ought to wait until they're of age. They're at their vulnerable times—nine, ten, eleven, twelve—when they're trying to find out their sexuality . . . and we're exposing them to this, and the studies show that if they're exposed to it there's a greater percentage of them that would be homosexual or bisexual," explained Texas State Representative Robert Talton (R-Pasadena). His point was that choosing to be gay when you're of legal age is "fine and good," but allowing gays and lesbians to become foster parents might unduly affect a young person's choice. His amendment prohibiting gay foster parents from adopting failed in April 2005.

"SOME OF US BELIEVE THEY WOULD BE BETTER OFF IN ORPHANAGES THAN IN HOMOSEXUAL OR BISEXUAL HOUSEHOLDS BECAUSE THAT'S A LEARNED BEHAVIOR. IF THEY CHOOSE TO BE HOMOSEXUAL OR LESBIAN, THAT'S THEIR CHOICE WHEN THEY TURN EIGHTEEN."

—Representative Robert Talton (R-Pasadena),
at the Texas statehouse, April 2005

Gray on the Concept

California Governor Gray Davis insisted on March 14, 2000, that judges he's appointed to the bench should "reflect the views I've expressed" or resign. "I've let every judge know that, while they have to follow the law . . . they're there because I appointed them, and they need to keep faith with my electoral mandate," said Davis at the National Governors Association conference in Washington, D.C., according to an article in the *San Diego Union-Tribune.*

"All my appointees," he continued, "including judges, have to more or less reflect the views I've expressed in my election. Otherwise, democracy doesn't work." Fortunately, the recall election in 2003 showed that democracy did work, and voters told Gray, "*Hasta la vista,* baby!"

A Conviction to Serve

★ ★ ★

According to an article in the February 11, 2002, *Louisville Courier-Journal*, among the candidates for county sheriff in Kentucky's May primaries, four were former sheriffs who had been kicked out of office after being convicted of crimes:

 Roger Benton (Morgan County)—
convicted of taking a bribe

 Paul Browning Jr. (Harlan County)—
convicted of conspiracy to murder

 Douglas Brandenburg (Lee County)—
convicted of obstructing justice

 Ray Clemons (Breathitt County)—
convicted for narcotics violations

Talk about your Kentucky Wildcats!

Jonathan Hunt, New Zealand's Speaker of the House of Representatives, ruled in May 2003 that though laptop computers are forbidden in Parliament, one member could bring in a carburetor and work on it as long he did it quietly.

The Doublemint Twins

Many people thought Ronald Blankenship, a shoe repairman in Birmingham, Alabama, was a shoe-in for sheriff during the June 2006 Democratic primary. But tongues started wagging when an article in the *Birmingham News* cobbled together some interesting facts from his past. It turned out that Blankenship was a real heel, having been charged with assault, passing bad checks, and faking his death in an insurance-policy scam. Blankenship, however, claimed his sole was pure and that it must have been another Ronald Blankenship who had done those terrible things—even though both Ronald Blankenships shared the same middle name and birth date and were married to women with the same first, middle, and maiden names.

"How many Palestinians were on those airplanes on September ninth? None."

—former Vice President Dan Quayle, MSNBC, April 30, 2002

He's a Real Blast

North Carolina resident E. H. Dennis (seventy-seven at the time) was found guilty in January 2000 of making a bomb threat during a 1998 Guilford County Commission meeting. The threat, caught on video, showed Dennis calmly describing how the commissioners' body parts would be blasted to the four corners if they didn't agree with him on a land-use dispute. During a break in his trial, Dennis left the courtroom and walked to the elections office, where he presented a $147 cashier's check as a filing fee to campaign for a seat on the commission. I certainly hope that as a member of the commission Dennis won't have a short fuse.

REPRESENTATIVE JOHN BOOZMAN
(R-ARK.) ALLOWED HIS DOMAIN NAME
BOOZMANFORCONGRESS.COM TO LAPSE,
SO FOR A WHILE, VISITORS SEARCHING FOR
INFORMATION ABOUT BOOZMAN FOUND
THEMSELVES AT A GAY PORN SITE FEATURING
"THE HOTTEST STUDS ON THE INTERNET."

A Defining Moment

In April 2003 the Oregon House of Representatives passed House Bill 2416, whose only purpose was to define the word "science" ("the systematic enterprise of gathering knowledge about the universe and organizing and condensing that knowledge into testable laws and theories"). It wasn't clear why the bill's sponsor, Representative Betsy Close, felt it necessary to legislate the definition—unless, of course, she's preparing for her next profession, as editor of *Betsy's Close-Enough Dictionary*.

IN THE 2007 FEDERAL BUDGET, $59 MILLION
WAS EARMARKED FOR MEDICAL RESEARCH
PROJECTS IN MULTIPLE HEALTH-RELATED
FIELDS, INCLUDING CANCER, DIABETES, AND
GYNECOLOGICAL DISEASE. ALTHOUGH I'M NOT
DISPUTING THE IMPORTANCE OF ANY OF THIS
RESEARCH, I AM WONDERING WHY THE MONEY
WAS SIPHONED FROM THE BUDGET OF THE
DEPARTMENT OF DEFENSE.

That's the Signpost Up Ahead

Before he left his position as an Atlanta city councilman in November 2001, Lee Morris attempted to vote through name changes for two small secondary streets. As a gift to his two youngest children Morris was going to designate the streets in their names, since they had complained that he had named a street after his other daughter six years earlier. Even after his constituents complained, Morris still tried to justify his intended actions by beseeching, "The only thing they ever asked from me was this." But voters contended that the street-naming scheme should be called No Way or Dead End or Back Off Boulevard. Eventually Morris recognized the warning signs and signed off.

Legistlation That Went Up in Smoke

Soon after Representative Roy Blunt (R-Mo.) became House majority whip in November 2002, he secretly slipped a provision into the bill creating the Homeland Security Department that directly benefited the huge tobacco company Philip Morris US by restricting low-cost cigarette sales on the Internet. Blunt's blunt smokescreen couldn't hide the fact that his campaign had received substantial donations from Philip Morris; his son is an employee of Philip Morris; and he recently wed the Washington lobbyist for Philip Morris. Blunt's attempt to cover Philip Morris's butt was so blatant that Tom DeLay had it field-stripped from the bill. After his provision was stubbed out, Blunt coughed out a reason why cigarette sales are connected to homeland security: he claimed that Hezbollah makes money by selling discount cigarettes. I'm not sure, but that sounds like a pack of lies to me.

Jim Lesczynski, a former Libertarian Party candidate for New York City Council, suggested in 2002 that the new tax on cigarettes would cause total havoc, create a violent black-market cigarette crime ring, and allow terrorist groups like Hamas to use profits from cigarette smuggling to finance their activities.

Finally, a Real Man of the People

"I enjoy cocaine because it's a fun thing to do. . . . I enjoy the company of prostitutes for the following reasons: it's a fun thing to do. . . . If you combine the two together, it's probably even more fun," stated Representative Robert Wexler (D-Fla.), parroting Stephen Colbert on the July 20, 2006, episode of *The Colbert Report*, during an interview for the "Better Know a District" segment. After other news outlets started running the interview and portraying Wexler in a bad light, Colbert lambasted them on the July 25, 2006, episode of his show and subsequently told his viewers to "vote Wexler," saying "the man's got a sense of humor—unlike, evidently, journalists."

On November 7, 2006, Wexler returned to *The Colbert Report* and joked about the now infamous interview. In response to Colbert's double-entendre question about whether he would "reach across the aisle" if the Democrats took back the House, Wexler, who understood the joke, said he'd learned his lesson about watching what he says.

Not Sure Who's the Nutty One

"You think you are big enough to make me, you little wimp? Come on, come over here and make me, I dare you. . . . You little fruitcake. You little fruitcake. I said you are a fruitcake," taunted Representative Peter Stark (D-Calif.), after Representative Scott McInnis (R-Colo.) told him to "shut up" during a legislative dispute in July 2003. This confrontation just proves the old point that nobody really likes fruitcake.

"PARENTS OUGHT TO BE THERE TALKING TO THEIR KIDS AND SAYING, 'YOU KNOW WHAT KIND OF FOOL YOU LOOK LIKE WITH AN EARRING? IF GOD HAD WANTED YOU TO WEAR EARRINGS, HE'D HAVE MADE YOU A GIRL..'"

—Alabama Governor Don Siegelman, September 2001

Putting the Fun Back in Fund-raising

In order to qualify for matching funds, New York City Council candidate Victor Bernace, a Democrat, needed to solicit at least seventy-five campaign contributions totaling at least $5,000. So in July 2005, he scheduled a "slightly sexy, naughty show to bring in voters" at a $20-a-head (no pun intended) fund-raiser at a nightclub. Because it's illegal to use campaign funds to hire erotic dancers, Bernace had to ask for volunteers—which temporarily made "stripper" a new staff position (pun intended). I'm sure the event raised more than just funds.

During the 2000 election for Anderson County, Tennessee, property assessor, candidate Bobby E. Jones confessed that he had served a prison sentence after being arrested on thirty-seven counts of making false statements to the federal government.

Where's Mr. Noodle?

It's not unusual for politicians to ask celebrities to speak to Congress about topics on which they are particularly knowledgeable or feel passionately. So when Representative Randy "Duke" Cunningham (R-Calif.) wanted to find an instantly recognizable superstar to speak on the importance of music education, he didn't go to Hollywood Boulevard or K Street—he went to Sesame Street. Cunningham asked the beloved, furry red creature Elmo to testify at the Capitol, and Elmo said, "Elmo be happy to." One political analyst who witnessed the event said, "Elmo has higher poll ratings than most members of Congress. They like to be in his reflective glory." At the end of his testimony, and before everyone got out their mat for a little nap, Elmo tried to convince people of his sincerity by saying, "Elmo is not making a mockery of this place." Granted, it's hard to take advice seriously when it comes from a felt puppet with someone's hand stuck up his butt.

Keeping It in the Family

Representative Bud Shuster (R-Pa.) supported a relatively unknown candidate to replace him in a special election in 2001—his son Bill Shuster, then a forty-one-year-old car dealer. Shuster used his influence to convince the Republican Party to divert funds into his son's campaign war chest until it reached an impressive $1 million (three times the amount reported by his opponent). "This is about Bill Shuster," Bill Shuster proclaimed, "and Bill Shuster standing on his own two feet." Shuster won the election and used his own two feet to walk up the Hill, where he can discuss his stalwart individualism with FCC chair Michael Powell (son of Colin Powell), Solicitor of the Labor Department Eugene Scalia (son of Supreme Court Judge Antonin Scalia), Health and Human Services Inspector General Janet Rehnquist (daughter of Supreme Court Judge William Rehnquist), Patrick Kennedy (son of Ted Kennedy and nephew of John F. and Bobby Kennedy), and, of course, President George W. Bush (son of—well, you fill in the blank).

Horsing Around

"The stallion approached, nostrils flared, hooves lifting with delicate precision, the wranglers hanging on grimly. . . . The stallion rubbed his nose against the mare's neck and nuzzled her withers. She promptly bit him on the shoulder and, when he attempted to mount, instantly became a plunging devil of teeth and hooves. . . . Greg clutched the rails with white knuckles, wondering, as these two fierce animals were coerced into the majestic coupling by at least six people, how foals ever got born in the wild."

—excerpt from the novel *A Time to Run* by Senator Barbara Boxer (D-Calif.)

America's Favorite Cookie

According to Vernon Robinson, a congressional aspirant from North Carolina, gay marriage will lead to "civil unions for three men, then four or five, then two transvestites, a pedophile, a lesbian, and a partridge in a pear tree." Vernon, an African-American, is legendary for his racially charged remarks, his outspokenness, and his offbeat ads, like the one in which he announced, "Jesse Helms is back! And this time he's black." One of Robinson's campaign pamphlets read, "Your vote could determine whether *VERNON ROBINSON* or my opponent—an admitted *NUDIST*—yep—like nekkid—like no clothes— represents the Republican Party." In another ad, Robinson reminded listeners about the difficulties liberals have in admitting that "black mothers need to stop having eight babies by seven different fathers, stop talking street-talk jive like 'Yo, dawg, peep my bling-bling.'" If Robinson were white he would be labeled a racist, but since he's black, he should be labeled . . . uh, a racist.

"If we have to, we just mow the whole place down,
see what happens."

—Senator Trent Lott (R-Miss.) offering a rather unorthodox Iraq strategy,
as quoted in the *Hill*, October 29, 2003

To Politicians Justice Means Just Us

When Randall Todd Cunningham was arrested for possession of four hundred pounds of marijuana in January 1997, surely his father, Representative Randy "Duke" Cunningham (R-Calif.), took the tough-love approach, right? Actually, in court the congressman who'd fought against "reduced mandatory-minimum sentences for drug trafficking" pleaded and cried for mercy, imploring that his son "has a good heart. He works hard. He's expressed to me he wants to go back to school." While Todd was out on bail, he'd tested positive for cocaine use on three different occasions; when a policeman had attempted to apprehend him during the third positive test, Todd had hurled himself out a window and broken his leg. Still, the congressman who supports the death penalty for drug kingpins was convincing enough to win his son a sentence of thirty months—half the federal "mandatory" minimum sentence.

Dude, Where's My Dad?

Josh Hastert, who used to own a record store called Seven Dead Arson, sported a goatee, and had a pierced tongue and ear, was hired by Podesta Mattoon, "a full service government relations and public affairs firm" (that is, a lobbying agency) in 2005 shortly after Josh's father, Dennis Hastert (R-Ill.), was made Speaker of the House. Josh promised that he would not lobby his father but did say he enjoyed his new job, because "doing consulting and government relations on the Hill took up a lot less time than running a record store and brought in a lot more money." Now that he's a lobbyist, that statement is probably the last thing that will be on the record.

Possessed and Repossessed

Rhode Island State Representative Joseph S. Almeida was convicted in February 2003 of assaulting a man who was legally repossessing Almeida's girlfriend's car. Almeida claimed he was innocent of the charges and that the repo man smashed his own glasses and mutilated his own face by voluntarily bashing his head into his truck's door three times. Apparently, Almeida gave the repo man a little extra face time.

"Not a single person told me we should debate about whether or not to have a debate on Iraq."

—Montana Senator Jon Tester on the Senate floor, relating what the folks back home have told him—or haven't told him, February 7, 2007

No, Not Ringo—the Other Starr

Kenneth Starr was the lawyer appointed to the Office of the Independent Counsel to investigate the death of Vince Foster, deputy White House counsel, and the Whitewater land transactions by President Bill Clinton. The Starr Report to Congress led to Clinton's impeachment on charges stemming from the Monica Lewinsky scandal. Starr had a lot of things said about him, but Congressman Mike Pappas (R-N.J.) went onto the House floor in July 1998 and sang about him:

> Twinkle, twinkle, Kenneth Starr,
> Now we see how brave you are.
> Up above the Pentagon sting,
> Like a fair judge in the ring.
> Twinkle, twinkle, Kenneth Starr,
> Now we see how brave you are.

Pappas's opponent ran this congressional concert on the radio during the 1998 campaign and succeeded in ousting Pappas. I wonder if this little ditty was Mike's way of moving into a second career as a 1990's reincarnation of the Mamas and the Pappas.

Duking It Out

★ ★ ★

Randy "Duke" Cunningham (R-Calif.) is known as an outspoken politician, but sometimes he just talks out of his ass, like when, at a public event, he discussed the rectal procedure he'd undergone as part of his prostate cancer operation. During the 1998 appearance, Cunningham said that it's "just not natural, unless maybe you're Barney Frank." Frank (D-Mass.), an openly gay member of Congress, rebutted by noting that Cunningham "may have suffered a little slight brain damage" during the anal surgery. Cunningham later gave a half-assed and nonsensical apology when he said, "I just get upset when people start bashing our military." The only bashing that went on was a little gay bashing by Cunningham himself.

Representative Lee Terry (R-Neb.) accidentally gave out the wrong 800 number to constituents looking for updates on the Medicare bill. The erroneous number connected callers to a sex chat line seductively answered with "Welcome to Intimate Connections."

Non-Sensenbrenner

★ ★ ★

The chairman of the House Judiciary Committee, Representative James Sensenbrenner (R-Wis.), lost his temper in the midst of sworn testimony during a hearing on June 17, 2005. He angrily pounded his gavel and abruptly ended the meeting where Republicans and Democrats were debating the renewal of the Patriot Act. Sensenbrenner ordered the court reporter to cease transcribing the proceedings and for the C-SPAN cameras covering the meeting to be turned off. According to House parliamentary procedures, meetings can be adjourned only by a motion or by the "unanimous consent" rule. But protestors found their arguments falling on deaf ears, as Sensenbrenner had already taken his gavel and stormed out and his staff had shut off all the microphones. Sensenbrenner reminds me of those obnoxious kids who, when they couldn't get their way, would take their toys and go home.

IN MARCH 2002, OFFICIALS IN FREMONT
COUNTY, WYOMING, PASSED AN UNBEARABLE
RESOLUTION PROHIBITING "THE PRESENCE"
OF GRIZZLY BEARS WITHIN THE BOUNDARIES
OF THE COUNTY. I HOPE THEY ALSO PASSED A
RESOLUTION MAKING IT MANDATORY THAT ALL
BEARS BE ABLE TO READ—BECAUSE
THIS PROVISION IS DIRECTED EXCLUSIVELY TO
THE BEARS AND DOES NOT MENTION
HUMAN INVOLVEMENT.

Unbridled Representative

An article in the June 9, 2004, issue of the *Roll Call* alleged that during a Republican delegation trip to Kazakhstan, Representative Denny Rehberg (R-Mont.) stayed drunk the entire trip, knocked back as many as twenty vodka shots before jumping on a horse, then fell off the horse and sustained a broken rib and several injured ribs when another horse trampled him. He was also accused of poking fun at the clothing worn by the Kazakhstan locals and of mocking them as Coneheads, flailing around and making beeping noises. Remulak, I mean Rehberg, called the editors of *Roll Call* to protest the story, saying he hadn't consumed mass quantities but had had only "three or four" shots.

Joseph Oliverio, while running for governor of West Virginia, admitted in February 2000 that he's had sixty speeding tickets and has been arrested more than 150 times for fighting.

Don't Go Ballistic, Man!

"This isn't rocket science here," explained Senator Thomas Daschle (D-S.D.), rejecting the idea of spending billions on President Bush's ballistic missile defense, also known as the "Star Wars" system, to a group of reporters on June 8, 2001. After a second thought, Daschle said, "Yes, it is rocket science, now that I think about it."

SUMPTER TOWNSHIP, MICHIGAN, SUPERVISOR ELMER PARRAGHI (SEVENTY-FOUR AT THE TIME) AND FINANCE DIRECTOR DWAYNE SEALS (THIRTY-FIVE AT THE TIME) COULDN'T GET ALONG AND WERE CONSTANTLY AND FEROCIOUSLY ARGUING WITH EACH OTHER ABOUT CITY BUSINESS. IN OCTOBER 2002 THEY EACH OBTAINED A JUDICIAL RESTRAINING ORDER AGAINST THE OTHER—EVEN THOUGH THEY BOTH WORK CLOSELY TOGETHER IN A FOUR-OFFICE BUILDING.

Burns—All Fired Up

★ ★ ★

Senator Conrad Burns (R-Mont.) went out of his way to arrive at the Billings Logan International Airport on July 26, 2006, in time to see a group of firefighters who were catching planes home. The Augusta Hotshots, from the George Washington and Jefferson National Forests in Virginia, had just spent more than a week fighting a ninety-two-thousand-acre fire and had finally contained it. Burns walked up to the firefighters and told them they'd done a "piss-poor job" and that they "should have listened to the ranchers'" concerns. He later complained to a Forest Service representative about one particular firefighter, saying, "See that guy over there? He hasn't done a goddamned thing. They sit around. . . . It's wasteful. You probably paid that guy ten thousand dollars to sit around." Burns was surprised to learn that the firefighters earn around eight to twelve dollars per hour. A notorious hothead, he had his fiery disposition doused in 2006 when his hot seat in Congress was extinguished.

"We thank God for those young people that do it every day and every night—to fight this enemy that's a taxicab driver in the daytime, but a killer at night."

—Senator Conrad Burns (R-Mont.) at a campaign event in Miles City, Montana, explaining his version of a day in the life of a terrorist, Associated Press, September 1, 2006

A Little Slap and Tickle

★ ★ ★

"Now I've seen what happened in Abu Ghraib, and Abu Ghraib was not torture. It was outrageous, outrageous involvement of National Guard troops from [Maryland] who were involved in a sex ring and they took pictures of soldiers who were naked. And they did other things that were just outrageous. But it wasn't torture."

—Representative Christopher Shays (R-Conn.) obviously realizing the true value of having a woman lead you around naked on a dog leash, in an October 11, 2006, debate with Democratic challenger Diane Farrell

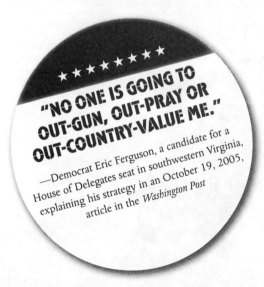

★★★★★★★★★★

"NO ONE IS GOING TO OUT-GUN, OUT-PRAY OR OUT-COUNTRY-VALUE ME."

—Democrat Eric Ferguson, a candidate for a House of Delegates seat in southwestern Virginia, explaining his strategy in an October 19, 2005, article in the *Washington Post*

One from Column A and One from Column B

On February 1, 2000, the city council of Boulder, Colorado, voted unanimously to add "gender variance," defined as "a persistent sense that one's gender identity is incongruent with one's biological sex," to the city's Prohibition of Discrimination in Housing, Employment, and Public Accommodations code. Employers, however, are required a "reasonably consistent gender presentation," as the code states that "a worker not change gender presentation in the workplace more than three times in any eighteen-month period." If you're curious about how one might permanently change "gender presentation," look no further than the ordinance defining "genital reassignment surgery."

In September 2003 the state of Texas began selling "Native Texan" license plates for a $30 annual fee. What isn't congruent with the Lone Star status, however, is that anyone in Texas can purchase the plates.

Dingell Bells, Dingell Bells

'Twas the week before Christmas and all through the House,
No bills were passed 'bout which Fox News could grouse;
Tax cuts for the wealthy were passed with great cheer,
So vacations in St. Barts soon would be near

—Representative John Dingell (D-Mich.) bustin' a rhyme on
December 6, 2005, regarding House Resolution 579,
which states that the House of Representatives
1. recognizes the importance of the symbols and traditions of Christmas;
2. strongly disapproves of attempts to ban references to Christmas; and
3. expresses support for the use of these symbols and traditions,
for those who celebrate Christmas

"To be very blunt, and God watch over Paul's soul,
I am a 99 percent improvement over Paul Wellstone.
Just about on every issue."

—Senator Norm Coleman (R-Minn.), as quoted in *Roll Call*,
April 7, 2003, positioning himself against Paul Wellstone,
the former Democratic Senator from Minnesota who died in a
plane crash on October 25, 2002

Puppies and Babies

In February 2002, Arizona State Representative Linda Binder (R-Lake Havasu City) proposed a law prohibiting unrestrained dogs from riding in the back of pickup trucks. Unfortunately, for the previous eighteen months Arizona legislators had attempted but failed to enact a similar ordinance that would cover unrestrained children in the back of pickups. Which might lead one to believe that Arizona has some damn fine dogs or some really rotten kids.

"If it were not for the strong support of the Jewish community for this war with Iraq, we would not be doing this."

—Representative Jim Moran (D-Va.) who immediately issued an apology to the Jewish community, March 3, 2003

Weapons of Mass-Media Destruction

"We have found weapons of mass destruction in Iraq, chemical weapons." This statement, uttered by Senator Rick Santorum (R-Pa.), were just the words the Bush administration, pro-war advocates, and many Republicans had been waiting for since the Iraq invasion on March 20, 2003. Santorum and Representative Peter Hoekstra (R-Mich.), chairman of the House Intelligence Committee, blew the battle horn on June 21, 2006, declaring that, according to a recently declassified report, five hundred chemical munitions shells had been uncovered since 2003. It seemed like the WMDs had finally been found. But it was quickly revealed that the shells were pre-1991 and that the agents inside them had degraded to the point of harmlessness—even the Department of Defense immediately countered they were "not the WMDs for which this country went to war." We're still looking for those.

"The illegals come over [the Arizona border] into the ranches. They kill their cattle. They rape their children. The children can't play in the yard anymore."

—Ezola Foster, vice presidential running mate to Reform Party candidate
Pat Buchanan, *Washington Post*, September 13, 2000

Just a Lucky Coincidence

★ ★ ★

In 2005, Representative Ken Calvert (R-Calif.) and his real estate partner Woodrow Harpole Jr. paid $550,000 for four acres of land a few miles south of the March Air Reserve Base in California. Less than a year after their purchase and without making any improvements to the land, they sold the property for $985,000. Why the sudden increase in value? Because $8 million had been earmarked by Congress to expand a freeway interchange sixteen miles from the property and an additional $1.5 million had been secured for commercial development in the area adjacent to the airfield. Who pushed for the earmarks? You guessed it: Representative Ken Calvert. I'm not connecting any dots here—I'm just telling you where the dots are.

ENVIRONMENTALLY CONCERNED OREGONIANS
WHO PURCHASED HYBRID GAS-ELECTRIC
AUTOMOBILES IN 2002 WERE GIVEN A SPECIAL
RATE WHEN IT CAME TO REGISTERING
THEIR CARS—THEY HAD TO PAY $15 MORE.
SINCE FUEL-EFFICIENT CARS USE LESS
GASOLINE, THE STATE MAKES LESS MONEY
IN GASOLINE TAX, SO IT RAISED THE
REGISTRATION PRICE TO OFFSET ITS LOSSES.

The Devil Made Them Do It

In an article in the November 17, 2003, *Dartmouth Review,* the reporter asked presidential candidate Robert Haines about the moral issues facing the nation and our churches, to which he replied, "Well the infiltration of the Church's body by the Dark Side okay? This is not by coincidence that all these things are happening. This is a deliberate attempt by the Dark Side to infiltrate the church . . . people working for Satan himself. Yes, the Dark Side, they are working for Satan. These people are not worshipping God, the most High, the most Almighty, or Jesus Christ. They are doing the work of the Devil—Satan himself." It always amazes me that people like this don't get elected more often.

"Well, you know, that's the problem in America, we're always having elections."

—Senator John Cornyn (R-Tex.) on the political dangers of Republican infighting on immigration reform during an election year, March 29, 2006

Pushme Pullyu

★ ★ ★

The wife of Representative John Doolittle (R-Calif.) can hardly be said to do little. During 2001-05, Julie Doolittle had at least three different jobs: she did event planning for Jack Abramoff; she served as the bookkeeper for a lobbying firm; and she worked as a fund-raiser, on commission, for her congressman husband. Her fund-raising company, based in the couple's home, has no phone listing or Web site, and Julie is the only employee. Because of the questionable nature of her business and her professional association with her husband, Congressman Doolittle announced in January 2007 that he would no longer employ his wife. A month later, the congressman announced that he still owed his wife nearly $137,000 and that his campaign was already in debt. Therefore, any contributions and fund-raising capital taken in during his 2008 campaign first went to paying his wife. The part that is scariest is imagining a man having to fire his wife.

Trashed and Trash Hauling

William R. Macera was reelected mayor of Johnston, Rhode Island, despite the fact that in October 2000 he and a campaign worker had been discovered at the Central Landfill in a car that police said heavily reeked of marijuana. Macera narrowly beat write-in candidate Louis L. Vinagro Jr. who had been arrested shortly before the election for threatening a state official inspecting his trash-hauling and recycling business. What's interesting is that Vinagro's business actually gives him a reason to be at the Central Landfill, but what kind of business was Macera up to there?

In August 2003 U.S. Representative Sheila Jackson-Lee (D-Tex.) complained to a reporter for the *Hill* that current names for hurricanes were too "lily white." Lee demanded that federal weather officials "try to be inclusive of African-American names."

Thanks for Nothing

★ ★ ★

To show his respect and gratitude for the citizens who voted him into office in November 2000, New Hampshire State Representative Tom Alciere (R-Nashua) went online on January 3, 2001, and posted that he'd been elected by a "bunch of fat, stupid, ugly old ladies that watch soap operas, play bingo, read tabloids and don't know the metric system." You'll be glad to know that in the September 12, 2006, primary for state senator, those same voters overwhelmingly elected Dennis Hogan in a write-in campaign, beating Alciere by an eight-to-one margin. Now Alciere has plenty of time to watch soap operas, play bingo, read tabloids, and learn the metric system himself.

"POLITICS HAS NO PLACE IN GOVERNMENT."

—Chicago Alderman Dorothy J. Tillman, on a local Sunday morning talk show, 2003

A Web of Confusion

"But this service [movies on demand] is now going to go through the Internet and what you do is you just go to a place on the Internet and you order your movie and guess what, you can order ten of them delivered to you and the delivery charge is free. Ten of them streaming across that Internet and what happens to your own personal Internet? I just the other day got, an Internet was sent by my staff at ten o'clock in the morning on Friday and I just got it yesterday. Why? Because it got tangled up with all these things going on the Internet commercially."

—Senator Ted Stevens (R-Alaska), explaining why in the tarnation all those Internets keep getting clogged, June 28, 2006

"I don't need Bush's tax cut. I have never worked a f—king day in my life."

—Representative Patrick Kennedy (D-R.I.) talking at a Young Democrats party at Acropolis, a D.C. nightclub, June 26, 2003

The Naked Truth

"The government should do all in its power to outlaw my pet peeves," said Georgia State Representative Dorothy Pelote (D-Savannah), and she'll help the government any way she can. On May 27, 2002, Pelote told her constituents that she'd be submitting what could be called a bare-bones bill—making it illegal to answer the door naked. She exposed the flaws in the existing nudity laws by stating, "The law allows [a person] to come to the door naked. It just doesn't let him go outside. I don't even want him coming to the door naked." I wonder if a committee made up of pizza-delivery boys and UPS guys was formed to protest Pelote's proposed bill?

During a June 2002 debate between Republican candidates for Alabama secretary of state, Dave Thomas angrily challenged opponent Dean Young to a fistfight.

One Hell of a Party

★ ★ ★

Senate Majority Whip Mitch McConnell (R-Ky.) buried a $20 million provision in a 2006 military spending bill "to pay for a celebration in the nation's capital 'for commemoration of success' in Iraq and Afghanistan." But since the United States wasn't successful in Iraq in 2006, the earmarked money surely went back into the general fund, right? Nope: the provision was extended so the president could spend the money in 2007, just in case. I'm not going to hold my breath waiting for my invitation.

"It's the most difficult [decision] I've made
in my entire life, except the one I made in 1978
when I decided to get a bikini wax."

—Arnold Schwarzenegger announcing his candidacy for California
governor on *The Tonight Show with Jay Leno*, August 6, 2003

Southern-Fried Crow

"Those are weasel words. . . . 'Compassionate conservative' is just like Al Gore talking about 'practical idealism.' They're designed to mean nothing. I think we need to say in plain words, 'I am a conservative.'"

—Republican presidential candidate Lamar Alexander, January 7, 1999

"I have come to admire and respect the term 'compassionate conservatism' because it defeated me badly in the Republican primaries in 1999. . . . So I think President Bush has given a good, clear definition of that and has done a real good job."

—Tennessee senate candidate Lamar Alexander, March 11, 2002

ACCORDING TO A SEPTEMBER 9, 2002,
ASSOCIATED PRESS ARTICLE, ROBERT
BOUSLAUGH QUIT HIS CAMPAIGN FOR SHERIFF
IN DURANGO, COLORADO, AFTER HE ALLEGEDLY
SHOT A MAN TO DEATH OUTSIDE AN ADULT
BOOKSTORE. BOUSLAUGH WAS LEAVING THE
ADULT BOOKSTORE DRESSED AS A WOMAN
WHEN THE MAN STOLE HIS PURSE. BOUSLAUGH
CLAIMED HE WAS "WORKING UNDERCOVER,"
BUT HE DID NOT GIVE ANY DETAILS.

Underwear Unaware

Mayor Don Wright of Gallatin, Tennessee, said he was supporting economic development by allowing an independent filmmaker to use his office on August 13, 2006, to shoot a scene for an upcoming movie. But everybody's panties got into a wad when the scene turned out be for the movie *Thong Girl 3: Revenge of the Dark Widow.* "They told me it was a film about a superhero woman and there was no nudity or any kind of offensive stuff in the film," Wright said. If Wright couldn't tell that a movie named *Thong Girl* might be a little risqué, he should have had someone brief him.

"Not a single person was marched into a gas chamber and killed."

—Representative Jeff Miller (R-Fla.), rebuking a group of Hurricane Katrina survivors at a congressional hearing on December 6, 2005, after they'd continually likened their temporary housing to concentration camps

Like a Bucking Coulter

"I'm happy to learn that after I speak you're going to hear from Ann Coulter. That's a good thing. I think it's important to get the views of moderates," noted presidential candidate Mitt Romney, introducing conservative writer Ann Coulter at the annual Conservative Political Action Conference on March 2, 2007. During her moderate speech Coulter said, "I was going to have a few comments about John Edwards, but you have to go into rehab if you use the word 'faggot.'" I would hate to see what Romney views as aggressive, wouldn't you?

NEW HAMPSHIRE STATE REPRESENTATIVE CHRISTOPHER DOYLE WAS ARRESTED IN MARCH 2003 AND CHARGED WITH ASSAULT FOR SLAPPING SIXTY-ONE-YEAR-OLD ELECTIONS SUPERVISOR GAIL WEBSTER AND KNOCKING HER TO THE FLOOR. DOYLE, WHO WAS RUNNING FOR TOWN SELECTMAN IN WINDHAM, STRUCK WEBSTER ON ELECTION NIGHT, RIGHT AFTER LEARNING HE HAD LOST THE RACE.

Forging Ahead

According to an August 15, 2002, report on CNN, Washington, D.C., Mayor Anthony Williams, a Democrat, was fined $277,000 for violating the city's election code. The election board had uncovered more than five thousand forgeries on the election petitions Williams had submitted for his candidacy. Among some of the forged names were Robin Hood, Robert De Niro, Wing Woo, Billy Joel, Tony Blair, and Kelsey Grammar. Apparently all these high-profile voters helped, because Williams went on to win the Democratic nomination.

The sheriff of Eddy County, New Mexico, was defeated in his reelection bid in July 2000. His name: Mr. Chunky Click.

Fat, Drunk, and Naked Is No Way to Go Through Life, Son

The New Mexico House of Representatives convened a special evening session on health insurance taxes in February 2004, but not all of the Democratic representatives were present. The Democratic leaders sent state police to a local hotel to bring back Representative Bengie Regensberg for the vote. According to the troopers, they had to subdue and handcuff Regensberg, who was "likely intoxicated," combative, and naked. But knowing how politicians are, I'm sure Regensberg was still allowed to vote.

"If I wanted to buy a bazooka to use in a very restricted way, to do something, I ought to be able to do that."

—Tom Coburn (R-Okla.) after the 1999 massacre at Columbine High School in Colorado, opposing President Clinton's proposal to make adults liable if they allow their children to buy guns and harm others

Dear Mr. Ben Dover

In concluding a February 15, 2006, letter written in response to a constituent's complaint about excess oil company profits, Jo Ann Emerson (R-Mo.), wrote, "Once again, thank you for contacting me regarding the testimony of oil company executives before the Senate Commerce Committee. Please feel free to contact me with other matters that are of importance to you. I am honored to serve as your Representative in the U.S. Congress. I think you're an asshole." Wow—an honest politician.

In 2001 the city of Dallas commissioned a study on doing business with local companies; the firm it hired to conduct the research was located in Oakland, California.

A Good Sport

On April 6, 2006, Senator John Kerry (D-Mass.) was busy proposing bill after bill, including S. 2574, making duty-free all "golf club driver heads of titanium, each with an aluminum hosel insert and a plasma welded face plate," and S. 2583, removing the duty on "basketballs having an external surface other than leather or rubber." In the spring, a senator's fancy lightly turns to what he's been thinking about all winter—outdoor sports!

In 1999 executives at Paramount Studios sent a cease-and-desist letter to stop Dallas Mayor Ron Kirk from "going where no man has gone before" by using the theme music of the TV show, *Star Trek*. Kirk's campaign ad began, "Four years ago, we chose Ron Kirk captain of the Dallas enterprise."